MEDAL OF VALOR

FIREFIGHTERS

Gripping Tales of Bravery from

America's Decorated Heroes

MI⟨ ⟩ **N**

Chicag   *ity*
Mil

2 104
PB
363
M

The *McGraw·Hill* Companies

Library of Congress Cataloging-in-Publication Data

Middleton, Michael L.
    Medal of valor firefighters : gripping tales of bravery from America's decorated
heroes / Michael L. Middleton.
        p.   cm.
    ISBN 0-07-141028-7
    1. Fire fighters—United States—Personal narratives.   2. Emergency medical
personnel—United States—Personal narratives.   3. Fire extinction—Awards—
United States.

TH9503.S44   2003
363'.3/7/092273—dc21   2003051465

This book is dedicated to the men and women of the fire service,
who willingly face death today to give someone a chance at tomorrow.

1 2 3 4 5 6 7 8 9 0   AGM/AGM   2 1 0 9 8 7 6 5 4 3

ISBN 0-07-141028-7

Interior photos courtesy of the individual firefighters and/or their families, except page
212, image copyright © Lawrence M. Browne.

McGraw-Hill books are available at special quantity discounts to use as premiums and
sales promotions, or for use in corporate training programs. For more information, please
write to the Director of Special Sales, Professional Publishing, McGraw-Hill, Two Penn
Plaza, New York, NY 10121-2298. Or contact your local bookstore.

This book is printed on acid-free paper.

CONTENTS

PREFACE

You didn't need an address to find the place; just drive toward the huge column of smoke and cinders rising into the night sky. People were jumping off the roof and out of the windows of the hotel, slamming into the sidewalk. A three-story fall to concrete looked better to them than burning to death. When I got there, it was a mess. The conflagration was consuming an old hotel that was in reality more of an apartment house. Forty years earlier, it had been a fashionable neighborhood, but now the street and the buildings were mostly just tired.

The firefighters were trying to go in the front door with hoses. An LAPD sergeant, Pete Durham, had a triage set up on the sidewalk in front of the hotel, and flames were coming out of nearly every window.

I was an L.A. police sergeant then, and we always rolled on fire calls, because, after all, we were all in it together. If you got hurt, who was going to come and scoop you up and take you to the hospital? Firefighters. When I was in the police academy, we were told that firefighters and their families were the same as cops, and if anyone didn't believe that, he or she should leave. Needless to say, we got on very well with the fire department. It was sort of a mutual admiration society.

I always knew that being a firefighter was just too damn dangerous. That's why I became a cop. No question, humans were never meant to go into burning buildings, climb up tall ladders, or do most everything else those men and women do; they just weren't. I was in awe of fire-fighters then and still am to this day. That morning at the fiery hotel, I was to see a new face of firefighters.

Sergeant Durham had his hands full, going from victim to victim. His motley crew was something to see. It looked like a scene from a B horror flick. Some were burned, others had compound fractures, and blood was everywhere.

"Petie, what do you need?" I yelled as I ran to him.

"I'm OK here. Check around back and see if anyone jumped. People are trapped inside too." Sergeant Durham was always cool under pressure. He was a U.S. Marine in Vietnam and later told me that while he was tending his injured flock that night, he had flashbacks to a battle he had been in.

Even though the flames were shooting out of the front of the building, preventing the firefighters from entering, they were making some progress. I knew they were going to go in very shortly. It was a noisy place with the diesel engines of the fire trucks and the pumps churning the water out, but you could still hear other sounds above the din.

Durham was right. People were trapped inside, and they were screaming. Death was at the door as I ran down the side of the building. I hadn't gone very far when I saw a young Latina woman at a window, waving her arms and calling for help in Spanish. "Help me! Help me! My God, help me!"

If the bars covering her window were the swing-away type, she could have easily escaped, but they weren't. Thick smoke was pouring out through the grates. The same steel bars that made her safe from intruders had turned her modest home into a jail cell.

I pulled on the bars, but they didn't move. I put my boot against the wall and pulled hard enough to lift myself off the ground, again to no avail. In an instant, the room turned to a deep red with tinges of yellow. The smoke was gone, replaced by fire. Like the stack from a blast furnace, fire shot around her shoulders and head. She screamed her last unintelligible utterance and was consumed by the swirling sea of flames that issued forth. The look of terror in her final moment as the room flashed over is scorched into my memory.

Three events can cause a room to suddenly be filled with flames: a flashover, rollover, or backdraft. A flashover occurs when there is already enough oxygen, and the temperature of the air and the contents of a room all reach the burning point at once. Then, everything in the room burns at the same time. A rollover is like a flashover, except only the smoke in the space has reached the ignition point. It is very short in duration and the smoke returns as soon as the flames subside. The contents of the room do not burn as in a flashover. A backdraft is created when the temperature of the air and/or the contents of the room have already become hot enough to burn but do not have the necessary oxygen to make it happen. When oxygen is introduced, such as when a door or window is opened, an explosive fire occurs. A backdraft can blow windows out or even the roof off a building. The rollover is the least dangerous of the three, but any of these events can kill a firefighter, even with protective gear in place.

The intense heat drove me away from the building. The screams subsided, and no more people appeared at windows as I made my way toward the back. Although I didn't know it, the firefighters had breached the wall of flames at the front door and were making their way down the hall with charged line.

In the back of the hotel, I was relieved to find no bodies. I decided to kick the rear door in and gain entrance in an effort to search for trapped victims. When I blew the door in with a monster kick, the fire answered back. Another blast of flames greeted me. Stepping back, I tripped and fell to the ground. The smoke was so heavy I could hardly see. I stood up into an electrical box, cutting my head and dazing me, which put me on the ground again. I then realized that the firefighters were gaining an upper hand somewhere in the hotel, because I was in about four inches of water on my hands and knees.

After that, I made my way back to the front to see if Durham needed any help. By then, the paramedics had taken over. They were also firefighters, and it was impressive to watch them tend to more than one victim at a time.

About thirty minutes later, the fire was fully contained and knocked down. The firefighters began to come out. When I had seen them earlier,

they had their game faces on. It was a battle, and they were totally up
for it. Now they looked so down. The fire had been beaten, but not
before it had beaten them. Several fatalities were inside the hotel, including the young woman I came face-to-face with. You could see it in their
faces; they lost. Not because the fire was too severe or because of any
number of factors that they had no control over. They had lost, and that
look penetrated their soot-covered faces. The pain of the victims was
their pain. Sergeant Durham and I both agreed—the look in their eyes
told the story of heroic warriors who were vanquished. They had died a
little that night too. The woman I had been face-to-face with was found
dead, lying only a couple of feet from the window where I had last seen
her. They expected victory, and the loss of life was a bitter outcome. It
is that indomitable spirit the stories that follow celebrate.

To learn more about, or to help, the kind of men and women you'll read
about in *Medal of Valor Firefighters*, check out these websites and
museums:

- *Firehouse* **magazine:** firehouse.com. *Firehouse* magazine has been
  saluting America's bravest for more than twenty years with the
  Firehouse Magazine Heroism and Community Service Awards
  program.
- **Hall of Flame Museum and National Firefighting Hall of
  Heroes:** hallofflame.org. Located in Phoenix, Arizona, this
  museum has almost an acre of fire history exhibits with more than
  ninety fully restored pieces of fire apparatus on display. The Hall
  of Heroes honors firefighters who have died in the line of duty or
  who have been decorated for heroism.
- **National Fallen Firefighters Foundation:** firehero.org. Created by
  Congress, the foundation leads a nationwide effort to remember
  America's fallen firefighters and is privately funded, depending on
  donations for its ongoing work.
- **FDNY Burn Center:** nyffburncenter.com. A nonprofit organization that strives to give burn care and treatment to all who need
  it. This valuable organization depends upon donations for its
  ongoing work.

ACKNOWLEDGMENTS

I wish to thank the following people for their generous help. Without them I could have never made this book a reality: the men and women of the fire service who lived these stories and their families, who allowed my intrusion into their lives; Harold Schaitberger, General President, International Association of Firefighters; George Burke, Assistant to the General President, International Association of Firefighters; Gail Walters, Director of Communications, International Association of Fire Chiefs; Liz Kirk, Promotion Manager, Motorola Corporation; Peter Matthews, Assistant Editor, *Firehouse* magazine; Dr. Peter Molloy, Executive Director, Hall of Flame; James Ward, Curator of Education, Hall of Flame; Chief Ronald Jon Siarnicki, Executive Director, National Fallen Fighters Foundation; Jolene Butts-Freeman, Public Information Officer, Atlanta Fire Department; Dale Whitaker, Public Information Manager, Austin Fire Department; Firefighter Steven MacDonald, Director of Public Relations, Boston Fire Department; Fire Chief Keith Barrett, Brookfield Township Fire Department; Deputy District Chief Dennis Gault, Chicago Fire Department; Barbara Becker, Human Resources Division, Columbus Fire Department; Battalion Chief Michael Fultz, Public Information Officer, Columbus Fire Department; Alan Etter, Public Affairs Officer, District of Columbia Fire Department; Jimmy and Vicki Carter; Captain Brian Jordan, Public Information Officer, Los Angeles County Fire Department; Captain Steve Martin, Public Education Captain, Los Angeles County Fire Department; Firefighter Specialist Raymond Rodriguez, Public Information Office, Los Angeles County Fire Department; Battalion Chief Robert Franco, Los Angeles Fire Department Community Liaison Office; Tim Bradley, Senior Deputy Commissioner of Insurance, North Carolina Department of Insurance; Captain Daniel Browne, Fire Department of New York City; Fire Chief Ed Wilson, Portland Fire Department; Fire Chief Walter Trapp, Port Washington Fire Department; Captain Bob Hennicke, Public Information Officer, St. Louis Fire Department; Sally Casazza, Office Manager, International Association of Firefighters San Francisco Local 798; Battalion Chief Mark Basque, Santa Rosa Fire Department; Paul Hart, Public Affairs Office, United States Forestry Service; District Chief Michael McNamee, Worcester Fire Department; my friend and agent, Gene Brissie, whose idea it was to do *Medal of Valor Firefighters*; and Michele Pezzuti, Ellen Vinz, and Rob Taylor at Contemporary Books, who shared the vision of a book that honored men and women of the fire service who were willing to risk every tomorrow they had so someone else could have one more. And last, but certainly not least, my wife, Martha, who listened to all the stories again and again and read every page with an editor's mind and red pen in hand. Thank you everyone.

1

SAFE AT HOME

October 17, 1989

San Francisco, California

Robert Boudoures and Gerald Shannon

If you loved baseball and lived in the San Francisco Bay area, this was a fantastic time. Not only was the World Series on, but it was a private party—no outsiders please. A Bay area duel was underway: Oakland versus San Francisco. The Giants were in a hole, down two games to nothing, but the boys were coming home and everything would be all right. More than sixty thousand fans were packed into Candlestick Park. They were certain nothing would stop San Francisco's powerful offense. They were wrong.

At 5:04 P.M., October 17, 1989, things began to happen. In San Francisco's Station 9, the game was on TV, and just as important, dinner was being cooked. Firefighter Gerald Shannon sat in the kitchen area talking to the man who had cooking duties that evening. "All of a sudden, things started to shake, I mean really shake. I was born in the city, so I know what earthquakes are; but this was different. I could see the parking lot,

1

This picture was taken while the rescue under the collapsed building was in progress.

and cars were just moving around. It was surreal. For a second, I thought my eyes were playing tricks on me, but they weren't. Then things got worse, and stuff started falling on the floor. The officer in charge came running in, and we went into an emergency mode of operation.

"The first order of business was to open the doors to the firehouse because it would be a huge hassle to get the doors up if the electricity went out. It was a good plan. We opened the doors, and the power went out. Then came the first of a long series of aftershocks."

Across town in Station 10, Captain Robert Boudoures and his men were out of the station almost immediately after the quake hit. They were answering a report of fire at a hotel. When they got there, the hotel staff told them it was out.

"Normally, we would have gone in and followed up, but not that day. All the way down, the radio traffic was crazy. There were calls for gas leaks, fires everywhere, and people who were stuck in elevators. I just grabbed the mike and reported that we were back in service. I knew it wouldn't take long before we got another call." He was right.

Back in Station 9, or "9s"—a common way for firefighters to refer to stations—Captain Mike Nolan told his crew to get the rigs into the street. Who knew what would happen with the next big aftershock?

Shannon drove that day and remembers what happened next. "We just started to circle the area around the station. We were up near Candlestick, which is about seven miles from the Marina area, and you could tell there was a lot of damage. On the radio, there was a lot of excitement. Usually guys are pretty low-key on the radio, but you could hear the tension in their voices. I knew we had big trouble on our hands. Buildings had collapsed, and people were dead. Things were really bad down there. I had been on the job for almost twenty years, and I hadn't seen anything like that before. This was definitely different."

Then came the call. Truck 9 was sent to the Marina. Captain Nolan looked at Shannon in disbelief. "They want Truck 9 to the Marina?" Back came the word, and they were off to the Marina. This meant that eighteen other ladder trucks were out of service, and because of the distance, Truck 9 would be the last one called to go there. No one else was available, and Shannon pointed his one-hundred-foot aerial ladder truck toward the Marina. Captain Boudoures was already on the way. Normally, five o'clock traffic is a mess, but not this day. As Shannon drove toward the columns of smoke rising from buildings in the Marina, cars pulled over and people waved them through one intersection after another. "You wouldn't believe how courteous everyone was. Maybe they couldn't do much, but this was their part. We were flying. One of the guys in the back told me to use the brakes.

"While we were en route, we got further orders directing us to a building collapse. As we crossed Lombard Street, you could see it lying in the street. The building used to be four stories, now it was a one-story pile of rubble. Fires were burning, but all the hydrants were dry; the water mains had broken." When the apartment house at the corner of Beach and Divisadero Streets collapsed, it did two things. First, the floors pancaked, one on the other; and second, it tipped over. The top floor ended up in the street.

Firefighters are tremendously resourceful. When I was a cop in L.A., we thought *we* were, but we didn't have a clue next to the boys and girls on the shiny red trucks. Because the hydrants had no water, one pumper went to the reflecting pools at the Palace of Fine Arts, laid a line to the collapsed building, and began supplying water to fight the fire.

The *Phoenix*, a fireboat, was dispatched to supply water to the Marina firefighters. Fortunately, it was high tide when the quake hit, and the boat was able to get next to the dock. They laid out five-inch lines and portable hydrants that formed the basis of the water supply network. Without it, additional lives would undoubtedly have been lost. Before it was all through, sixty-three people had died, and nearly four thousand were hurt in what was, at the time, the most costly natural disaster in America.

Captain Boudoures and his crew, Firefighters John Carvajal, Joe Conway, and Jim Jenkins, pulled up to the collapsed building. Residents at the scene told the captain they'd heard cries for help from under the building. Boudoures had Porter, Conway, and Carvajal check for possible victims at an adjoining partially collapsed building.

Boudoures and Jenkins searched the building where cries for help had been heard. "Jenkins and I started removing debris, but there was no way to get back to the victim. After a few minutes, we came out and tried to locate gas lines feeding the buildings, to shut them off."

When 9s arrived, some of the firefighters joined the search of the adjoining building. It was painfully obvious that anyone in the collapsed building was now dead. Nothing was left of the block-long building. It looked like a demolition site after a structure is dropped and before it is hauled away. "Some fatalities were in one of the other buildings, and we were waiting for the coroner to come. Some other people were hurt too," Shannon said. "I was watching this guy from Pacific Gas and Electric Company [PG&E]. He was checking the pile, I guess for gas leaks. Then he came over to me.

"He said, 'I think I heard someone under there.' "

" 'Under there?' "

" 'Yeah.' "

The first thought that came into Shannon's head was, Shit! If someone is under there, how would you get in to find him?

Shannon talked to Boudoures and learned there was someone under the building. Shannon said he wanted to check it out and was told, "OK, go ahead and check it out, but do not go in there."

"So I went over and started looking. I didn't think I would see anything, let alone hear someone." The chance of the PG&E worker hearing anything was nearly impossible because of the high noise level in the area. Buildings were burning and fire trucks were parked in the street with their engines running, in addition to the nearly constant din of air traffic on the fire radios.

"I looked in through a window under a planter box. Just think of it, a window was under the flower box and not the other way around. I yelled, 'Anybody in there?' Then a voice came back to me.

"It said, 'Yeah, I hear you.'

"I yelled back, and sure enough, the PG&E guy was right."

Captain Boudoures was out of his truck and had his men check the buildings for people trapped inside. Then, he saw smoke coming out of a building. He had learned from the PG&E employee that the collapsed building had a gas leak, and it was not safe to be around it. He also saw Shannon looking into the twisted mass of broken lumber calling for sur-

vivors. Shannon looked back and said, "Hey, you know Bob, I think I
hear a voice in there."

Boudoures replied, "Well, you're not going to be able to get in there,
and if you do and there is another aftershock, we'll never get you out."

Nonplussed, Shannon responded, "Yeah I know, but I'd like to give
it a shot." Boudoures just looked at him and said, "Well, go ahead."

Shannon describes what he found. "I started crawling in. Everything
was out of place. What I thought was a floor was a ceiling and it was so
strange. I kept calling out as I headed in. I told the voice to keep calling
and I would try to follow the sound. We both kept yelling to each other.
I had a flashlight with me, and I just kept going in. Then, the path came
to an end in a mass of wood. There was nowhere to go."

Normally, firefighters work in turnout gear, which is a fire-resistant,
insulated, canvas-looking fabric that is a lifeline of protection. Their helmet is another source of protection from heat and falling objects. When
the air is smoky or dangerously poor, they wear a self-contained breathing apparatus (SCBA), also called a Scott Pack. A firefighter may also
wear a Nomex hood to protect his or her face, neck, and ears from the
heat and flames. The opening in the front of the hood is covered by the
SCBA facepiece, which is made of a black rubber product and has a high-
temperature-resistant, clear plastic window to look through. Shannon
wore none of these. He had no room to maneuver in the tight confines
of what was passing as a hallway. It was so small, he could only crawl on
his stomach.

He could now tell it was a woman's voice he had heard. It was time
to discuss the situation. He returned to Boudoures and said, "She is in
there; I can definitely hear her."

"OK. Let's get some shoring, blocks, and wedges. We can build it up
to make sure you have a way out if something happens," Boudoures
replied. As in nearly every fire operation, this was a team event. Firefighter Jerome "Duke" Polizzi volunteered to join the other two men and
they entered the building to start the rescue, Shannon leading the way.
The other firefighters would maintain the framework to protect
Boudoures and Shannon. Firefighters take calculated risks to save lives.
Without Polizzi and the other firefighters backing them up, this would

have looked like a suicide mission. If something went wrong they would be there to rescue the rescuers.

Robert Boudoures had a note of caution for Shannon. "Keep your light on, and I will try to stay in visual contact with you as you go. If anything happens, it's going to happen fast." At that point another firefighter, Ron Lewin, crawled under the pile and offered his help. Captain Boudoures stationed him at the entrance. There wasn't enough room for anyone else. If it all went south, Lewin would assess the situation and begin to rescue the rescuers.

Shannon headed back to try and find another path. Captain Boudoures was behind him. Once again, he reached a point where he could go no farther. Shannon called out, "Captain, I need a chainsaw." The call was relayed back to the opening, and a saw was obtained. When the PG&E man heard Shannon's equipment request, he warned them that the use of the saw was dangerous because of the gas. Periodically, there were flame-ups in the pile of rubble, which had now begun to burn. A rescue is always an event with only a limited amount of time, but the clock had just sped up.

An adjacent building collapsed, sending a mass of flaming embers spilling over the rescue site. Shannon and Boudoures worked inside and knew nothing of the newest danger to them. Later, all of them would describe their mission as single-minded. They blocked out everything that wasn't part of the job at hand, whether it was shoring, delivering needed equipment, clearing debris, conferring on beams to cut, or actually cutting them. Everyone under the pile was "in the zone."

Crawling forward on his stomach, Shannon began to make his way to the trapped woman. As he inched forward, he held the saw in front of him, cutting as he went. As he progressed, he passed the wood he cut back to Boudoures, who in turn relayed it back to the other firefighters behind him. Shannon could hear muffled conversation above him, and the news was not good.

"Guys were talking on top of the pile, saying that I was running out of time. The gas company guy was very worried. He told Captain Boudoures that it wasn't safe for us to be under there. It sounded like he wanted us to be ordered out. He said that I could cause a spark with the chainsaw and it could ignite any gas that was leaking. There was no way we could leave. Once you make contact with someone who needs your help, you can't just leave him or her behind. If we were to leave, she would die; Bob and I knew that wasn't going to happen. It wasn't just us; it was Duke, Ron, and Rich as well. We made a commitment, and we were going ahead with it. The PG&E man was right about the gas because I could smell it too. I was hoping he was wrong about the saw and the gas.

"We were making progress, and I just kept talking to her. After a while, I was able to hear her voice clearly, and we started talking to each other. Of course, when I had the saw going, I couldn't hear myself think. And the fumes were bad; the whole area was clogged with smoke from the saw, and it wasn't good. I just kept talking to her, though."

"What is your name?" Shannon asked her.

She replied, "Sherra, Sherra Cox."

"I'm Gerry. Don't worry, we're going to get you. Just hang on."

"You won't leave me, will you? I don't want to stay here, don't leave me behind."

To reassure her Shannon said, "Not a chance."

In reality, there was a chance she might not get out. She might not be pulled to safety, but they weren't leaving the building without her. One of two things was going to happen. Either they were all going to crawl to safety, or they were going to die in that dark place that only an hour and a half before had been her new home. Shannon continued his conversation with Sherra.

"What were you doing when it hit?" he asked.

"I was walking down the hall when it started shaking. I stood in the doorway to my bathroom, just like I learned in grammar school. And then the walls collapsed. Somehow I ended up on the floor or one of the walls with the door on top of me. It has my hip."

As Shannon cut his way past what was formerly Sherra's bedroom, he could see what used to be her four-poster bed. It was now partially holding the ceiling up from the floor.

"You know, I just moved in here. I was still unpacking my dishes. And all my opera records were still in boxes. They're here somewhere."

The fire was now moving in on them. It was burning beneath the surface and impossible to stop. With the water supply from the harbor now in place, they no longer had a water shortage. But now, water was flowing down in a virtual torrent into Sherra's face. Boudoures told them to shut down the hoses.

Captain Boudoures told Lewin to bring in an inch-and-a-half line, which was then passed up to Boudoures. He used it to extinguish the small fires as they popped up. The cutting, prying, jacking, and shoring continued. Lewin also directed the shoring operations. It had been more than two hours, and they still had a long way to go, maybe a lifetime.

This was clearly the closest any of them had been to not making it. Anxieties were high. They were all scared, but more than that, they were firefighters on a rescue mission. Boudoures watched as Shannon cut each piece of wood. This was a life-and-death game of pick-up-sticks. If the wrong beam were cut, everyone's fortunes would take a turn for the worse.

Outside, in the waning bit of daylight, the news media had gathered. This was a big story within a bigger one. It was transmitted live on television to millions of viewers, including those at the Shannon residence. "Mom, do you think Dad is in there?" Confidently, his wife responded, "If he is, he won't take any chances."

By now, Shannon could see Sherra. It didn't look good. She was smashed by so much wood, and he stopped his saw. "It got so bad, I don't think I could have cut butter. I told her I had to go back for another saw."

Sherra pleaded, "Gerry, please don't leave me. Don't go."

"I'm going to be right back with a new saw." He touched her hand. "I'll be right back."

Sherra Cox had been the best. Even though she was seriously hurt, she didn't complain. This was the first time she displayed any panic at all. "Don't go."

"I have to, but I promise you this, we're going to be having coffee in an hour." Sherra didn't seem as confident as Shannon. Actually, he wasn't so sure either, but he had no intention of sharing it with her. Before leaving, he gave her a flashlight to ease her mind. She was going to be alone for a short period, but she wouldn't be in the dark while she waited.

When Shannon got back with the new saw, he continued to cut and remove beams and debris. It wasn't long before the saw refused to cut. The sharp teeth had been flattened after repeated contact with nails. Another saw was needed. This time Captain Boudoures would make the saw run. When Boudoures got back, he shared some troubling news.

He said, "Gerry, the PG&E says it is getting worse with the gas. I think we better work as fast we can. The clock is really ticking."

It had been over two hours since the first cuts were made. Armed with a fresh saw, Shannon went back in and began cutting again. He wondered if their luck hadn't started to run out.

It was now time for the last of the cuts to be made. Shannon looked at the beams, studying them carefully. Captain Boudoures and he talked about what needed to be cut. The fire was now closing in on them. It was a red glow, eerily visible in the dark. Shannon tried not to think about what was beyond the light. He had more than enough to worry about. Again the heavy smell of gas came over them. Then a distant "whoosh" as it ignited.

Suddenly the ground shook again. The world above them dropped, but only six inches and stopped. It was cramped before, but now Shannon could barely raise himself up off the floor before hitting the wood above him. They had to get out and it had to be right away.

He said, "Sherra, I'm going to give you something to cover your face with. I'll be cutting some pieces that are really close to your face and I don't want anything to hit you."

Lieutenant Rich Allen had responded to the scene after the rescue had started. He was also a paramedic. It was decided that he would make an assessment of Sherra Cox before they attempted to extricate her. The newly cut path was a one-person lane, so Shannon had to move out of the way so that Allen could move into position. He conducted a careful examination of Sherra. With the violent nature of the collapse, she could have easily suffered spinal injuries. Allen was pretty sure all she had was a crushed pelvis. That was bad enough, but her injuries could have been much worse.

Allen moved past Shannon and told him they needed a backboard for her. He crawled the forty feet back through the makeshift tunnel. Then it was show time.

Shannon had blocked the outside world from his thoughts as he marshaled all his power and knowledge in meeting the greatest challenge of his career, but now he was at a crossroads. He paused as he waited for Allen and reflected on his life. "I thought about my wife and my kids and how important they were to me. I knew there was one more big cut to make. I just didn't know what the outcome was going to be. I was certain that Sherra wasn't coming out of there if I didn't do it. The big question in my mind was would any of us come out, alive at least. It wasn't just me; it was for her, Bob, Rich, and Duke. This cut was for all of us."

The red glow was on them by now. It had been two and a half hours since they started the rescue. Shannon carefully studied the beam and discussed it with Captain Boudoures. Then it was time. "I started the saw up, laid it to the wood, and it was done." Nothing moved except the piece he wanted to cut.

"Sherra reached out and grabbed my hand. She didn't want to let go. She couldn't believe it either. Rich crawled in with the board. She was in a lot of pain when we moved her on it, but she just bit her lip and didn't say a word. We didn't even take the time to strap her down, we just went.

"I pushed and Rich pulled and out we headed and for the first time, she let out a couple of cries. As we left, I saw just how much the fire had grown. The whole wall on one side was orange. We were out of time.

"It was so strange when we came out. When I went in, it was sunny and now it was dark. We were under there for two and a half hours. In some ways it flew by, and in others it seemed like forever.

"There were all kinds of floodlights on. Every television station in the city was there. When we got out, someone else took charge of the backboard, put her on a stretcher, and rolled her to the ambulance. I didn't want any part of the news crews. I just ducked into the shadows."

Then he heard, "Hey Shannon, is that you?" He looked up at another firefighter and smiled. "If I had known it was you under there, I'd have let it burn." They both laughed.

Sherra Cox got to the ambulance on the stretcher, but refused to let them put her in. She wanted to talk to Shannon first. Summoned by nearly everyone, he walked to the ambulance. As he approached, she smiled at him.

"I gotta have your name, your whole name," she said.

"Shannon."

"An Irishman. I was rescued by an Irishman." Sherra reached up and grasped his hand and pulled Shannon down. She hugged him and said, "You're my hero."

As he watched the ambulance pull away, Shannon watched the lights and thought back on the last three hours. It was a good feeling.

For their actions that day, Captain Robert Boudoures, Firefighter Jerome "Duke" Polizzi, Lieutenant Richard Allen, and Firefighter Gerald Shannon were each awarded a Class A Meritorious Award for their individual and collective action in volunteering to undertake the saving of a human life under the most adverse conditions and at extreme personal risk.

In addition, Shannon was awarded the Scannell Medal and Boudoures the Sullivan Medal, the highest awards for valor given by the San Francisco Fire Department. Shannon was named as the Firefighter of the Year in the United States by *Firehouse* magazine. The magazine's Heroism and Community Service Awards are the result of a national search wherein any fire department can submit firefighters for consideration. The magazine receives hundreds of nominations and a council of firefighters meets and considers the nominations before making the awards. The Heroism and Community Service Award program is the largest in the nation.

The World Series resumed almost two weeks later. The Oakland Athletics swept the Giants four games to none.

2

A WALK TOWARD THE WATER

August 27, 1995

Mebane, North Carolina

Gregg Hinson

During the afternoon of August 27, 1995, nearly eight inches of rain fell in about two hours on the small town of Mebane (pronounced MEH-bin), North Carolina. Meteorologists described it as a three-hundred-year-rain event. Not only were the streets flooded with water, but the fire department was too—with calls. The volunteer department had been out on back-to-back calls. One was for a flooded basement, the other for an overflowing culvert that threatened some homes. That much liquid had no place to go, at least not for a while.

About two miles from town, a car was stranded in the water on a bridge. The bridge crossed a creek that was normally five feet wide and perhaps two feet deep. Engine 33 was at the culvert call with Engine 32. Gregg Hinson was on Utility Rescue 34 in the station. His first name was actually James, but everyone called him by his middle name, Gregg. Assistant Fire Chief Tim Bradley was on 32.

Gregg Hinson, Mebane, North Carolina, Fire Department.

It was decided to leave 32 at the culvert call in town to make sure there was coverage for the next call. Bradley and Hinson responded in separate trucks to Highway 119 where it crossed over Stag Creek. All of the creeks were now raging torrents. The following day, in another part of town, a woman and a girl were found dead in a car twenty feet up in a tree. Their vehicle had been washed over the side of the road by the waters.

Hinson's unit arrived at the location just ahead of Bradley. A car was stuck in the water that was rushing over the bridge, and a man was sitting in the driver's seat. The water was up to the bottom of the passenger-side windows. The road sloped down to the bridge then back up again on the other side. As the two men looked down at the car, water flowed from right to left. The area that was flooded was about 250 feet across. Where the car sat, the normally two-foot-deep creek was more than thirty feet deep under the bridge. The speed of the water on top of the bridge was not ultrafast, but beneath, however, it was a different matter. As the water came out of the other side, it was boiling. Chief Bradley was experienced in rope rescue. He was the North Carolina deputy state fire marshal and had trained in rope rescues for some time.

Back near the trucks, Hinson, along with Firefighters John Schultz and Keith Buckner, prepared for a lifeline rope rescue. When they saw Bradley, who had arrived by himself, they called to him to come down to them. He jogged down, looked at the car in the water, and asked about the driver, who had been yelling that he was trapped.

Bradley listened to the firefighters' plan as he studied the area. It was going to be important to have a place to secure the rescue line. Because of the high water, it wasn't possible to tie off on the upstream side. Quickly he made a decision. "Move 34 down and let's tie off to it. Then let's rig a braking system for the rope on the front."

The men planned to string themselves out on a line. Hinson was to be in the lead with Schultz and Buckner following behind at five-foot-long increments. They were clipped onto the rope with harnesses.

Once Hinson entered the water, he would have to walk about 125 feet to get to the car. Bradley studied the scene as they all walked toward the water. Before they started, he stopped them.

"Gregg, I want you to stay on the right side of the car. Don't go down-current from the car, no matter what you do."

"OK."

"When you get even with the car, then you can move down to it. Come in on the upper side and let the water carry you down to it."

They all nodded as Chief Bradley spoke.

"The car has moved a little to the left, so let's watch it very carefully. If we see something that doesn't look right, we'll tell you."

Then Bradley advised Assistant Chief Todd Bradley, who was the overall incident commander, of the plan and how they were going to implement it. Tim Bradley entered the water with the three other fire-fighters. He knew he was not going to command from dry land. He stayed upstream from the others. "Pay attention guys; it looks like the water is coming up a bit." The force of the current had also increased as the water on top of the bridge became deeper.

The rushing of the water through the trees and over the bridge created a lot of noise. The driving rain had subsided to a mere drizzle by now, which was a small blessing. At least they wouldn't have rain pelting their faces.

Hinson was now almost even with the rear of the car. Chief Bradley was in roiling water just above his knees monitoring the rescue. As he moved forward, Hinson called out to the driver.

"Sir, we are going to get you out. Come over to the right side of the car. We are going to take you out that way. Move over to the passenger side."

Just then, Buckner lost his footing and grabbed a tree limb for support. Bradley watched as he regained his balance. "Hey Keith, you need some rocks for your pockets?"

Hinson was now above the passenger window of the car. "Sir, come over to my side. Come over to me."

"Gregg, what's the holdup?" asked Bradley.

Hinson replied, "Chief, he won't budge."

"Tell him if he doesn't move over so you can get him out, we're going to leave him. We don't have a lot of time here. The car is moving."

By now, the water was almost chest deep, and the current was stiff. Hinson again tried to get the driver to cooperate. "Sir, we've got to go. Come on! Come to me and I will pull you out."

He still didn't move, but Hinson wasn't going to give up. He yelled to the others, "I can get him. I'm going to move down by the car and get him."

The car was moving slowly toward the edge of the road, pushed by the ever-increasing strength of the water. Hinson was walking with it, moving in on his prey. If the car went over, it would drop into thirty-plus feet of thrashing water.

When someone is going to jump from a ledge, you move slowly and get into a position that will allow you to tackle him and pull him back. It was that way for Hinson. He knew if he told the driver he was going to snatch him out of the car, he would have to contend with an altercation. That was the last thing either of them needed.

Hinson made his move. His upper torso disappeared into the passenger window. He grabbed the man around the chest under his arms. Hinson's tactic worked. Out came the man's head, then his shoulders, his waist, and then his feet were free. He was out of the car.

"You've got him, Gregg. Hang on to him." Bradley was elated that Hinson was able to accomplish such a feat under very adverse conditions.

Bradley watched what happened next as though it were in slow motion. The car went over the bank and was sucked into the torrent. Without the car to block the flow of the water, the current surged, sweeping Hinson off his feet. The water washed over Hinson's shoulders as he tightly held the man. Then his helmet was blasted off, and they were both gone, swept away, sucked into the same swirling water that had just eaten the car.

Schultz and Buckner were behind Hinson, along with Chief Bradley. They were all pulled down and moved through the water toward the edge of the road. Schultz and Buckner were pulled over the side of the road. Bradley knew if he didn't let go of the line he would go over as well. The chief knew he had to think very quickly.

"My mind was racing. Get a grip to stop yourself. I was being pulled down into the current by the force of the water. I had a flash of the image of Gregg just before he was blown off the road, and I thought I was going to be next. I realized the only thing I could do was turn loose of the rope. If I held on, they would be trying to rescue me. My only thought was to get myself upright. I was almost out of air, but I was able to surface and get to my feet."

Once upright, Bradley yelled to the crew on the rope brake to hold the tension. Then he told them to start hauling the rope back to them. Then the line hung up. He couldn't see Hinson at first, but he could see the other two. Then more bad news. He saw Hinson's boot surface and saw that he was facedown. Still, they pulled on the line, not realizing they couldn't free Hinson because he was tangled in a telephone pole's guy wire, which his safety belt had hooked on as he washed by.

The rope was coming back and with it, Schultz and Buckner. They were all right. Immediately, firefighters were in the water and worked to free Hinson. It took about five minutes before he was brought to shore. Paramedics were waiting to start working on him. Very quickly, he was on his way to the hospital.

After the driver had been pulled from the car, he was swept free when he went over the edge. He ended up in a large clump of trees, where he hung on until he was rescued a second time.

No word was heard from the hospital. They had started working on Hinson immediately, and Bradley knew there was a chance for his friend and fellow firefighter. In the apparatus bay at the station, the firefighters cleaned and stowed their gear. It was very quiet. Bradley remembered that anyone could have heard a pin drop. They were going through the same motions they had so many times after a run, but this time it was so somber. Some of them cried quietly as they worked. Others stared in silence. Still no word came from the hospital.

The phone rang. Captain Jay Smith took the call. Gregg Hinson was gone.

He is the only Mebane firefighter to have ever been killed in the line of duty. His wife, Lisa, was at church when word came. She and her two children would never again enjoy the life they had before that terrible rainstorm came to their little community.

A few years later, Mebane built a new fire station. It was named the Gregg Hinson Memorial Fire Station. A couple of Christmas seasons after his death, the department held a Santa Claus party for the firefighters' children. Lisa Hinson and her children were there. One of the firefighters came up to Chief Bradley and said that a man wanted to talk to him.

"I went out to talk to him, and it was the man Gregg had saved. He was crying and said he wanted to talk to Lisa. She agreed and came out to talk to him. He was crying and hugged her. Afterward, she said she felt better about things.

"There just wasn't any doubt that without him being pulled from the car, he would have drowned. The car ended up three hundred feet from the bridge and was destroyed."

Gregg Hinson was honored posthumously with a Medal of Valor by the governor of North Carolina, and was also awarded a Medal for Valor by *Firehouse* magazine as part of their Heroism and Community Service program.

In many ways, Gregg Hinson and the rescue on the bridge exemplify firefighters in a larger sense. He was called to help someone whom he didn't know. He had trained for this type of event and willingly put himself in harm's way. Then suddenly, the situation changed and not for the better; but he didn't give up. Even when the man he was trying to rescue was too frightened to follow directions, he still didn't call it quits. And then, in the blink of an eye, Gregg Hinson was gone. But, make no mistake, if called upon to do so later that same day, the firefighters who had just watched their friend make such a sacrifice would have waded into fearfully dangerous waters to save a life. That day it was water, but it could have just as easily been a fire.

3

FLASHOVER

January 5, 2000

Austin, Texas

Alphonse "Ax" Dellert

The call came early in the morning on January 5, 2000. Austin Fire Department Engine 6 got a call at 5:30 A.M. for a fire at an apartment complex at 2213 South Lakeshore Boulevard. Without giving much information, the caller hung up. Often, people will call the police or fire department and excitedly state where and why a unit or truck is needed. But then they hang up before the dispatcher can obtain fill-in information. Engine 22 was the primary company and Alphonse "Ax" Dellert's Engine Company 6 was to respond as a backup unit.

"On the way to the call, I was wearing my full turnout gear and pulled on my SCBA. Then I pulled up my Nomex hood and secured my helmet. This was an apartment fire, and it was the middle of the night. I thought it was highly probable that we would find trapped people inside. Just as we got there, we got word that the fire was contained. I walked over to Engine 22 to say hi to the guys. I really could have taken off my

Alphonse "Ax" Dellert, Austin, Texas, Fire Department.

SCBA and pulled down my hood, but I was feeling a bit lazy and thought I would just leave it on until we got back to the firehouse.

"The crew from 22 had already made an entrance on the second-floor apartment where the fire originated. I was standing there and I noticed fire starting to show through an exterior wall. There is a saying that if something can go wrong, it will. Well, in this case a bunch of things went right."

A section of three-inch hose had been brought up to the location near the apartment by some other firefighters. Firefighter Specialist Bruce Callan was the acting lieutenant on Engine 6. He noticed the hose had not been charged (filled with water). He told Dellert that he couldn't get anybody on the radio, so he was going to walk back to the engine where the line had come from and have them take care of charging it.

A ladder was leaning against the wall of the apartment. Earlier, it had been used by a firefighter to climb up to a window and break it to vent the fire, which is done to lower the heat in a building, let the smoke out, or control the flow of the flames. If the flow of the fire is routed in a particular direction, then the firefighters can set up and fight it in there, rather than letting the fire choose its own path.

A hose bundle was sitting on the lawn next to the ladder. A bundle is two folded hoses with nozzles used to connect to the three-inch line if needed. It allows firefighters to hook up two-and-three-quarter-inch lines to have additional firefighting capabilities immediately. If the bundle was not needed, it could be put back on the truck.

Dellert describes what happened next. "As soon as Bruce left, the whole second floor flashed over. Flames went everywhere, out all of the windows. There was a lot of noise and now the whole upper part of the apartment was totally involved in flames."

Then Dellert heard a voice pleading, "Help me. Help me. I'm burning up."

"I had no idea who was talking. There wasn't anybody missing, but I knew I heard something. I was standing about twenty feet from the apartment and the same distance from the engine. This voice didn't come over the radio, and there wasn't anybody standing near me."

Considering that Dellert was wearing a Nomex hood and he was standing very close to a pumper truck with its engine running, it was very unlikely that he could hear anything, even from someone standing a few feet away. Without hesitation Dellert ran to the ladder and climbed up halfway. He stopped and listened.

"I turned off my radio and listened. I heard the voice again. 'Help me, I'm burning up.' "

If someone was trapped, time was short—very short. He jumped off the ladder and put on his facepiece.

"Once I had my facepiece set and my air was turned on, I grabbed the hose bundle and took out one of the inch-and-a-half lines. If Bruce hadn't gone back to charge that line, if the hose pack wasn't there, if the window wasn't broken out, if the ladder wasn't there, and if I had taken off my gear when we were told the fire was secure, then I would not have gone anywhere."

But it was all there. Dellert looked up at the window. The heavy, black smoke that had been pouring out was gone, replaced by a three-foot by three-foot column of flame that rolled out of the missing window, which was where he was heading. With hose in hand, he went up the ladder.

"It was hot, like a blowtorch when I got up there. I turned on the hose to drive the flames back. I used a fog stream [the finest spray position on the nozzle] to try and kill the flames. When the fine spray entered the room, it was converted to a blast of steam that knocked the flames down instantly. It also had the effect of lowering the temperature in there, which I hoped would stop another flashover from occurring. I hooked the nozzle on the window and climbed in.

"As soon as I got in there, everything went red. The room flashed over again. Any good I had done by spraying the room was over. The flames got me real good. I thought for sure that I had lost one of my ears and part of my face. It was a good thing I hung the hose in the window, because I turned around and grabbed it. I was able to drive the flames back once again.

"I couldn't see my hand in front of my face. There was heavy, black smoke—pitch-black. To my left was the living room, which was fully involved in flames. Flames were pouring out of the living room and into the bedroom. Toward the left, it was as bright as the sun, while on the right, it was as dark as night."

Dellert decided to use an angle setup for his search. "Since I couldn't see anything, I didn't want to just move around in the room. I decided to head straight in. I was calling out to see if anyone would answer back. I was kind of crouched down as I went, and I spread my hands out to the side trying to feel for someone as I went."

Again he heard the same voice call out, "Help me, I'm burning up."

"I couldn't understand how anyone could still be alive in that room, but they were and speaking so calmly. The voice wasn't screaming or panicky-sounding at all. I started moving to where I heard the voice."

In the darkness, Dellert saw a sliver of light playing across the floor. He crawled to it and pointed his own flashlight in the direction of brightness. Reaching down, he found a turnout coat worn by Captain John Butz. Until that moment, no one had known the captain was missing and in terrible trouble.

Captain Butz was one of the initial firefighters inside the apartment. His Ladder 35 crew arrived first and found the fire on the exterior of the apartment. They knocked it down and everything seemed fine. They didn't realize that it was really an interior fire that had only burned through to the outside. Butz and his tailboard man, Firefighter "Big Al" Thompson, entered the apartment and found that the smoke had pushed all the way to the floor. Smoke and other heated gases naturally rise, but if the smoke has nowhere to escape, it will then fill the room and will eventually extend all the way down to the floor level. When smoke is pushed down toward the floor, firefighters refer to it as being "banked down." Usually, a little clear air is on the floor that allows a firefighter to look ahead and gain a sense of his surroundings. Not this time. Captain Butz told Thompson to get a gasoline-powered smoke-ejecting fan. He then put his SCBA on and reentered the apartment.

Firefighters learn a technique called either a "left-hand pattern" or "right-hand pattern" search. Staying in a low, crawling position, Butz executed a right-hand pattern search for anyone who might still be inside the apartment. Placing his right hand against the wall, he began to search the room with his left. Because in these situations the firefighter can see nothing and the search area is totally unfamiliar, touching the wall greatly decreases the chance of getting lost. Thousands of fire victims, who couldn't find their way out of buildings, are found only a few feet from safety. Captain Butz was protecting himself from that fate. Also, when any given search is completed, it is usually simple to turn around and use the other hand against the wall to find the way back out.

He went through the kitchen. Nothing. Next he checked the den and moved on to the bedroom. After inspecting the perimeter of the room, Butz left the wall to check the bed and when he got near it, the entire apartment suddenly flashed over, driving Butz to the floor. He didn't move from that place as the flames swirled around him. Within a few seconds, his face shield melted, and his turnout gear, subjected to temperatures of more than two thousand degrees, blackened as the severe heat began to attack his skin. Outside, standing next to the fire truck sixty feet away, Dellert heard a call for help and began to act.

"I couldn't believe a firefighter was in that room. His voice was so clear and calm. It's very hard to talk and be heard by someone wearing a facepiece standing right next to you. I just didn't understand how I was able to hear him and no one else did. I knew for sure neither one of us had much more time left in that room."

Captain Butz was lying facedown on the floor. All of his protective gear, though damaged, was still in place. Dellert knelt down and spoke to the captain.

"Come on buddy, I got a window over there. Let's get out of here."

Dellert helped Butz to his feet. Staggering, the two men began the arduous ten-foot journey to the window. With his hand on Captain Butz's back, Dellert steadied him as he walked.

"When we got within five feet of the window, I could see a silhouette. The very first light of day was showing on the horizon and it was backlighting Firefighter Rip Esselstyn. He was standing at the top of the ladder using the hose I had left on the window ledge. That was another thing that went right. He had kept the room from flashing over again. When we got to the opening, I tried to get John through the window, but he was fighting me. He later said he was afraid I was going to drop him. I was having a hard time with my hands by then. They were so badly burned I thought I lost both my thumbs. Even though the room had cooled a lot, it was still several hundred degrees, and I was really having trouble."

At the window, Esselstyn was having problems as well. He saw Dellert go in through the window so he followed him up the ladder. When he looked in, the blast of heat caused second-degree burns to his face.

As he moved him through the window, Dellert told Esselstyn to take the captain.

"Have you got him? Do you have Captain Butz?"

"Yeah, I have him," replied Esselstyn.

Butz was in very critical condition by this time, and he was disoriented. He acted as though he couldn't go through the window for fear of injury. If the captain didn't go through the window, Dellert couldn't save himself. Esselstyn pulled Captain Butz through and held onto him as best he could. Unfortunately he lost his grip and both men fell to the ground. Luckily, the captain was not injured in the fall.

The heat in the room was rapidly accelerating again. Dellert dropped to the floor to escape further burns, realizing that he could not use the same ladder. Esselstyn and the captain were still lying on the ground. If Dellert fell, he could further injure them.

"I felt along the wall and found another window that was broken out. I couldn't take the heat anymore. It was so incredibly hot in there, and for the first time I was fearful that I might not be able to get myself out if I waited any longer. When I looked out, I remember seeing the sky. It was a pale blue. I grabbed the edge of the window and pulled myself through it.

"In a matter of a second I went from a room that was about a thousand degrees into the crisp morning air that was just about at freezing temperature. In that split second I didn't care what was at the bottom. Whatever it was had to be better than that room. I had seen a patch of green and decided to aim for that. I reasoned it would offer some cushion to my landing.

"When I was flying through the air, the cold felt so incredibly good. Out of my left eye, I could see a patch of green coming up really fast. I was relieved that I was going to hit my target. Then I slammed into the ground. My first thought was, My God, I've made it. Then came the pain. Not from hitting the ground, but from the burns I had suffered. I pulled off one of my gloves and with it came most of the skin. I was so shocked as I looked at my disfigured hand. I had just started my life as a burn victim."

The only person left in the apartment was the twenty-three-year-old man who lived there. He was found in the bathtub, dead. He probably became disoriented as he tried to escape the flames and went into the bathroom by mistake, where he died of smoke inhalation. If he had kept going straight out from the bedroom, he would have made it to safety.

Other firefighters rushed to the aid of their three injured comrades. Even though Esselstyn had second-degree burns to his face, he remained at the scene fighting the fire. Firefighter Luis Gutierrez ran to Dellert. When he pulled the facepiece off his comrade, he was shocked. He later told his friend that with all the soot and burns to Dellert's equipment it didn't even look like him, and he couldn't tell who it was at first. Dellert was just one blackened lump in what used to be turnout gear.

Dellert was transported alone to the hospital in very serious condition. Shortly after his admission, he was sent to a burn unit in San Antonio for two weeks. He suffered deep second-degree burns to his face, both ears, the left side of his neck, and one of his calves. In addition, he underwent extensive skin-graft surgery to repair some of the damage to both of his arms.

Captain Butz was burned even more severely. There were second- and third-degree burns to more than 53 percent of his body. He had more than twenty skin-graft surgeries and had the large toe on his left foot removed and reattached to his left hand to replace the thumb he lost in the fire. He spent two months in the burn center and is still being seen as an outpatient.

Remembering back to the fire, Captain Butz said he tried everything he could to get out of the room after the flashover. "It was so hot. I wanted to get up, but I couldn't move. The next thing I knew, Ax was there, telling me we had to leave."

After being off duty for eighteen months, the captain returned and is now working in the training division. When asked if he thought he paid a big price for being a firefighter, he said, "It's just part of the deal."

For his actions, Alphonse "Ax" Dellert was decorated with the Medal of Valor from the Austin Fire Department. He also received medals of valor and heroism from the American Legion in Austin, who made him their firefighter of the year. He was also Firefighter of the Year for the Southern United States American Legion. The Military Order of the Purple Heart, Texas chapter, decorated him with a Purple Heart. Finally, he was chosen as Firefighter of the Year by *Firehouse* magazine as part of their Heroism and Community Service program.

People often ask Dellert how, with all of the surrounding noise and with his Nomex hood on, he was able to hear Captain John Butz at such a distance. "I don't really know. I do know that I heard him as clear as a bell. They all tell me that when we have on our hoods and facepieces we can't hear each other five feet away. I know it's true. I don't know what to say other than he was as clear as a bell. His voice and flashlight drew me directly to him.

"I think his guardian angel and mine must have gotten together and said 'We gotta get together and help these guys.' They did a good job.

"I've thought a lot about that call, thinking about whether I should have gone in there. If I didn't go in, how could I face my kids? If I didn't, what would I say if they asked me, 'Aren't you supposed to go in and save people at all costs?' "

Dellert is back on the job at full duty.

4

FIRE IN THE SKY

April 12, 1999

Atlanta, Georgia

Matthew Moseley

The Fulton Bag and Cotton Mill, at 170 Boulevard Street, was a long-time fixture in the Cabbagetown district, an old part of southeast Atlanta. The mill building was constructed in 1881 and had been in operation for almost one hundred years when it closed in 1977. Now it was slated to become a complex of 150 apartments. Similar mills in the area had already been transformed into housing units. The old neighborhood was getting a new lease on life. Mill Building Number One was the hub of a spokelike pattern of structures. The restored buildings were to become the centerpiece of the new Cabbagetown retail district.

On April 12, 1999, the transformation project to turn the abandoned mill into an apartment complex was still underway. It was a clear day with temperatures in the seventies, but it was very windy. The fire started when a saw being used somehow ignited the contents of a trash can. At 2:40 P.M., a call was dispatched for a structure fire at the old mill. Res-

Matthew Moseley, Atlanta Fire Department.

cue Squad 4 had just returned to the station after responding to what turned out to be a false alarm for a chlorine spill at a doctor's office.

When the Cabbagetown call came in, several units were dispatched. Atlanta firefighter Matthew Moseley of Rescue Squad 4 was with one of them. With the number of units being dispatched, he figured that there was something to this call. Moseley and the other firefighters were on the truck and out of the station in less than a minute.

"We left the station and were getting dressed in the truck on the way to the fire. We hoped we would be back before too long. Some of the guys were talking about the dinner menu at the firehouse for that evening. When we approached the fire, we could see it was a big one and that we were going to be there for a while."

Several units arrived at the same time as Rescue Squad 4. Moseley and several other firefighters were sent to check out the progress and exact location of the fire. At the time, this building was the largest historical renovation in the country.

Neither the sprinkler system nor the standpipes (used to supply water to the building for use in a fire) were in place yet. Standpipes enable the firefighters to hook up several inch-and-three-quarter lines on every floor. Water pressure is maintained by a pumper, with a hydrant being the primary source. At the Fulton Bag and Cotton Mill, all of the lines would have to be pulled up by hand.

The building was brick construction on the outside and heavy post and beam on the inside. The main beams were six by six inches. As Moseley and the other firefighters got to the fourth floor, they were greeted by the ominous sound of the beams on the floor above them popping.

"We started running down the stairs. When we got to the third level, back over my shoulder I could see the black smoke and fire and the floors collapsing. I can say that was a time that I did not expect to make it out. When we got to the second floor, the fourth and fifth pancaked onto the third. We were staying just ahead of the collapse.

"Then, when we got outside, we realized we had a missing man. Lieutenant Mark Greene was not with us. We weren't sure where he went.

Somebody said he had gone out a different door. We went back into the building to look for him, but we only made it up to the second floor. We were driven back by the fire. It was all going to come down again.

"I went back outside to figure out how we were going to find Mark. The area where we thought he might have gone had collapsed. There was a collapse of the parapet wall, and it was just a pile of bricks now. We all started picking up bricks to find him. I thought he was going to be under there.

"Some of the other firefighters were trying to get him on the radio without any luck. Then he answered back. It seemed he had come out of the building and found that the truck was about to be consumed by fire. So, he was moving it. The Plexiglas was melting along with the steering wheel and the rotating emergency lights. He actually drove off with the hoses still attached. This isn't standard practice, but it was either that or lose the truck."

By this time, the building was almost totally involved in flames. The fire had gone from nothing to disastrous in only a few minutes. When Assistant Fire Chief Joe Tolbert arrived, the question in his mind was, "How many firefighters have just been lost?" It wasn't even a question of "if." The answer, thankfully, was none.

The winds were whipping embers away from the mill, and several nearby homes were on fire. Moseley, along with several other firefighters, was assigned to fight those fires. Because of the size of the fire, they faced a critical shortage of water. Near the mill fire, there was a tremendous amount of air being pulled into the base of the fire, which created an incredibly strong wind and made the flames rise high above the building.

Moseley walked back to the truck for an additional assignment and noticed that everyone was looking up. A construction crane was positioned high in the air beside the burning mill, and the crane operator, Ivers Sims, was moving about in the cab.

Earlier, Sims had noticed a small fire but was unconcerned, thinking it would be put out directly. Within a few minutes, he saw fire trucks arrive and was certain they would be able to extinguish the growing blaze. However, in just moments, forty-mile-an-hour winds fanned the small fire into a major conflagration. The fire grew so rapidly that Ivers could not get down. He was trapped 225 feet in the air.

Then, a call came out over the radio for Moseley's squad. "It was a rope rescue somewhere, but I didn't hear where. I thought that there was no way they were going to send us downtown for some rescue when we were at the biggest fire in Atlanta in twenty years.

"There wasn't going to be any need for us to go downtown. The rescue was right there. While we were involved with the spot fires caused by the blowing embers, several plans were being considered to get Ivers Sims down.

"The prevailing consensus was an air rescue that had to involve a helicopter. A television news helicopter circled overhead, but with all of the equipment it carried, a delicate rescue was out of the question. The police helicopter unit was not configured for such an attempt."

A helicopter was available with a top-notch pilot, Boyd Clines, a Vietnam veteran who had flown many dangerous missions. The helicopter belonged to the state and was operated by the Department of Natural Resources and Department of Transportation. Clines's copilot and navigator was Larry Rogers, and they were also experienced mountain rescuers.

The first thought was to use a rescue basket suspended below the helicopter. That was scrapped when someone expressed the valid fear that Sims might panic and fall to his death.

The news media helicopter had landed, and Moseley was sitting inside the chopper discussing possible rescue methods with the pilot. Moseley was up for the try. The plan involved a firefighter sitting on the landing strut, controlling a rope. Another firefighter would descend to Ivers on the rope and pick him up. Moseley and the pilot decided against this plan when the firefighter who volunteered to control the rope said he didn't know if he could handle the weight of two people on the line. Then, the plan was revised to have an additional firefighter inside the helicopter to hold onto the one on the strut. Moseley didn't like the idea, but was willing to give it a try.

"It was time to go. I was expecting the crane to topple from the heat at any moment. We had to do something. Just then the Department of Natural Resources helicopter flew overhead and I saw this big ring underneath it. I knew right then this is what we needed."

Moseley's lieutenant, Bill Bowes, looked up at the helicopter at the same time, and the two men looked at each other. "He was thinking the same thing I was. Whoever got to the helicopter first was going. When the other helicopter landed, I jumped out as fast as I could. Bill had his seat belt on and had a few more obstacles to overcome than I did so I made it to the helicopter first."

"I still thought the best way was to go up there inside the helicopter and then rappel down to the area of the crane where Ivers was. By this time, Ivers had left the cab and retreated back to the area where the large counterweights were located.

"I told Clines my plan and he looked at me and said, 'OK, if you want to take the ride.' I had no idea what he was talking about. I was wearing a rescue harness with my turnout gear over the top. One of the things I was concerned with was the heat, especially on the harness.

"The copilot came to me and said to come with him. I'm all ready to get into the 'copter, but we were not walking in that direction. I told him that I wanted to get my stuff rigged up. He said to me, 'No, you're not going to need that.' I was thinking, What's this guy talking about?

"Then I understood. There was about eighty feet of rope laid out in front of the 'copter. That's what Clines meant by 'take the ride.' I was going to be dangling under the 'copter."

The rope was a one-inch nylon cargo rope. Matthew Moseley inspected it carefully for cuts and frays. His life and Ivers's depended on it.

"I was standing there, hooked to the line in front of the helicopter, and Captain Doyle came out to wish me good luck. They told me to walk toward the 'copter when it lifted off so I wouldn't get jerked off balance. And I did."

Moseley carried with him a twenty-foot piece of flat nylon webbing to make a harness when he got up there. As gently as could be, he was lifted off the ground. Millions of Americans would later watch what happened next, as it became a national news story. Atlantans saw it live. Sharrin Jenkins, Matt's fiancée, was also watching. She knew it was him, recognizing his new fire gloves immediately.

"It was the most fearful, terrifying thing I'd ever done. After I got up into the air, I looked out over the city. I could see eight or nine columns of smoke from fires started by the mill fire. Some of them were a half a mile or more from where I was.

"In the air, I remembered the words of Geronimo to his braves going into battle—it was a good day to die. Well, I thought, for a firefighter, it was a good day to die.

"It was a calming thing to be up there, because the anticipation was gone. Now the fear was replaced by the knowledge that I had a job to do.

"We flew past the crane once. Boyd was trying to get the best read on the fire, wind, and the crane. If I got hung up on the crane, all four of us were dead. I don't remember the wind, the sound of the helicopter engine, or the noise of the fire. All I remember was the intense focus on what I had to do.

"Boyd started to slow down as we made our approach. Larry was Boyd's eyes as far as what I was doing. I had no ability to communicate with them."

The heat was not significant when they were circling. It was a different matter when Moseley approached the crane. The metal was so hot that Sims's shoes were melting. The blast of heat hit Moseley, and he was forced to tuck his face into his turnout coat for protection.

Now he was only a few feet from Sims. The crane operator yelled at him to watch the deck, but Moseley didn't know what he meant. He saw black marks on the white platform. He didn't know that they were caused by the melting rubber from Sims's shoes.

"I was really concerned that he would lunge out to grab me. So I made it clear to stay put and I would come to him. He did that."

Clines wasn't happy and made another pass. Moseley had a major problem. He had gotten turned around and was now facing away from the crane deck as they made another approach.

"There was nothing I could do. I couldn't see anything. Then it was like the hand of God gave me a push because for no particular reason, I rotated around. There was the deck of the crane and I just stepped onto it." It was the most gentle of approaches as Moseley landed. The helicopter pilot now had to hold a steady position in a forty-mile-an-hour wind while Moseley prepared to take on a passenger.

"I didn't know what to say to him. I know that sometimes a little humor can lighten up a tense situation. So I said, 'Hi there. Well listen, your boss sent me up here and he said it's OK for you to knock off early today.'"

Sims just looked at him and said nothing.

"It went over like a screen door in a submarine. I don't think he found any humor in my comedy routine. Here he had waited all this time, and they sent a comedian up to rescue him. I figured I would just stick to my rescue work.

" 'What's your name? Mine's Matt.' With that, I made the harness and hooked him up to it. About two weeks before, I had gone to an instructor's conference, and we trained on making this exact harness. The timing was great."

The helicopter never moved. Moseley had a couple of extra feet of slack in case there was a gust of wind or some other unexpected event. Time was running out, and the helicopter engine was overheating. Inside the aircraft, intense heat was radiating up from the fire and melting the helicopter's plastic windshield. For Moseley and Ivers, the large concrete counterweights were actually cool in comparison.

Then came the signal, thumbs up. The slack disappeared and up the two men went. As though it were nothing, Clines flew them out of harm's way and put them on the ground. Thirty minutes later, Moseley was on the phone with the vice president of the United States. Al Gore said the same thing everyone else who saw the rescue said: "That was, well—just amazing."

Later that night, Sharrin met Moseley at the fire station. She put her arms around him and hugged him very tightly as she whispered into his ear, "I'm so proud of you."

Matthew Moseley was awarded several medals for valor. They included the International Association of Fire Chiefs' Benjamin Franklin Fire Service Award for Valor, which is cosponsored by Motorola Corporation; the [Atlanta] Metropolitan Fire Association Medal of Valor; the City of Atlanta Fire Department Medal of Valor; the state of Georgia Governor's Public Safety Award; and one of the top awards for heroism from *Firehouse* magazine.

Ivers Sims later commented about Matthew Moseley, Boyd Clines, and Larry Rogers on national television: "God bless them for the rest of their lives. Thank God for giving them the ability to do what they did yesterday."

5

WORKING FROM HOME

June 30, 1991

Chicago, Illinois

Raymond Caballero

It was 5:45 A.M. on June 30, 1991, and in fifteen minutes Raymond Caballero's life would change forever. Caballero was a Puerto Rican kid from the projects of Chicago. Many of his boyhood friends had chosen a different path. Caballero heard the Chicago Fire Department was going to be testing and applied to take the test. "Before I heard they were testing, I never really thought about being a firefighter. I know a lot of men and women on the job who always wanted to be a firefighter. I almost stumbled into it, but I've never regretted it."

This particular morning he was asleep in bed with his wife, Maria, as a fire spread in the house next door at 4447 West Wrightwood in the city of Chicago. Caballero's neighbor, Vivian Syberson, was sleeping peacefully as a fire in her home grew.

Bang! Bang! Bang! Bang! Bang! Bang!

Raymond Caballero, Chicago Fire Department.

"I was asleep one moment and, with the pounding on my door, I was awake the next. I knew for sure that something was wrong somewhere."

Bang! Bang! Bang! Bang!

Caballero jumped out of his bed. He was wearing nylon running shorts and pulled on a pair of work shoes. Looking outside he could see his next-door neighbor. She was screaming that her house was on fire and her mother still inside.

"I'm coming down," Caballero answered. He turned to Maria and told her to call 911.

"What's going on?" she asked.

"The house next door is on fire. Call the fire department too." Even though the 911 call would result in fire department communications being notified, Caballero wanted the responding firehouse to know exactly what they were facing upon their arrival.

He ran down the stairs, wiping the sleep from his eyes. As he came out, Vivian's daughter met him and said that her eighty-two-year-old mother was trapped in their burning home.

"Where does your mother sleep?" Caballero asked.

"She has her bedroom."

"Where is it? Is it closer to the front or back of the house?"

"In the front of the house, on the second floor."

After finding out from the daughter that the front door was open, Caballero ran toward the house. As he got to the front door, he could see smoke billowing out and over the top of the doorjamb. He dropped down to his hands and knees and approached the front door.

"I knew there was a fire, but I didn't know what would happen when I opened the door. If there was going to be a backdraft, or if the house was going to flash over, I wanted to be as low as possible.

"I stuck my head into the entrance into the house and saw another doorway up a flight of stairs. Inside, I could see the smoke building up, and it seemed to be coming from the bedroom area. On the left side of the door I could see flames coming through.

"I crawled in farther. I figured this was where the lady must be. When I got to the next doorway, I pushed it open. I could see Vivian on the bed. There was fire everywhere in the room. She was moving—quivering."

Caballero assessed the challenge he was facing. Flames were coming up from under the mattress, which was on fire on all sides. The flames were traveling up the walls and had ignited the curtains as well. The only protective clothing he was wearing were nylon jogging shorts and work shoes with no socks. Maria had telephoned 911, and the fire department was coming, but for Vivian to have any chance at survival, action had to be taken immediately.

Very little smoke was in the room. Instead, there were flames, and the heat was extremely intense. Caballero watched as flames broke through the mattress.

"I was starting to become disoriented from the heat. I made my first attempt to grab her, but she slipped through my arms when I tried to put them around her body. The flames were coming out and burning me. She kept sliding away from me. It was so hot.

"I went back to the floor again to consider what to do. I noticed her legs. I thought I could get hold of her ankles and pull her that way. I had to get her off the bed. She was literally burning up right in front of me.

"I raised up again. I didn't realize my skin was burning. I was just thinking about saving her. By then, at least 80 percent of the room was on fire.

"I grabbed one of her ankles and started pulling her off the bed. I lost my grip and fell backwards about three or four feet. I hit the wall next to a window and got tangled in the curtains. I got burned pretty good then because they were all on fire. I pulled myself free and in the process fell again. This time I landed on the floor on my butt. When I looked up, I saw the wood around the door that I had come through had caught on fire.

"I made another attempt to get her off the bed. I lost my grip on her again and fell backward and landed on something that was on fire. I rolled off onto the floor. The flames were about six inches high where they were coming through the mattress.

"I knew it was now or never. This was it. I said to myself, I have to do this and I have to do it now. I grabbed her ankles and I started pulling. I just kept pulling. I was kind of hunched over. I couldn't stand up, it was just too hot."

As Caballero pulled, Vivian fell to the floor and lay on her back. At least he had gotten her away from direct contact with the fire. He began to pull her by her arms, which were extended over her head. Inch by inch, Caballero slid her along the floor.

Near the door, Caballero hit an obstacle. One of Vivian's legs had become entangled in a chair, which caught on the doorjamb. He was through the flaming threshold, but couldn't get her past the chair.

"I thought, Oh shit! What am I going to do now? She was stuck between the chair and the doorjamb. I couldn't pull her legs free because they were burned so badly and I couldn't get a good grip on them.

"For the first time I started to think I was going to pass out. While I wrestled with the chair and her, my left side was making direct contact with the fire. I still never thought about how serious this situation was. I didn't realize the danger I was in. I just saw her in there and thought I could scoot in and get her and get out. I thought I would just grab her, but then there was all the heat and the flames started to lick her body and I was feeling light-headed. If I passed out in there, we would both be dead. I just wanted to get her out."

He was finally able to free Vivian from her entanglement with the chair. By that time, the room was totally involved in flames. The heat had taken its toll. When the brain and nervous system are subjected to severe temperatures, things stop working correctly. Ray was becoming disoriented and operating on pure adrenaline. He moved Vivian out of the doorway and over to the edge of the stairs.

"That was it. I hit the wall and couldn't go anymore."

Although he didn't know it, Ray was critically burned by the time he ran down the stairs and outside. Five or six people from the neighborhood were watching.

He yelled, "I need some help!"

Nobody moved.

"Help me! Somebody?"

Nobody stepped forward. They were frozen in fear. Firefighter Raymond Caballero was faced with the reality that if he didn't take action Vivian would die. It was clear that it was all up to him.

He ran back inside and up the stairs. The fire advanced again and was now on top of Vivian. Caballero grabbed her by the ankles and pulled her slowly down the stairs, on her back, to the walkway outside. The first Chicago fire unit had not arrived yet.

Vivian Syberson was now free of the fire. Caballero knelt over her as she lay on the walkway. She was not breathing.

"Once I realized she wasn't breathing, I opened her mouth to check for obstructions. I didn't find any, but her mouth was black as shoe polish. Looking at her clothes, I could see the damage the fire had done to her. It was like they were tattered. Not completely burned away, just sections gone.

"I gave her seven or eight chest compressions and blew into her a couple of times. She started breathing right away. It wasn't regular, but at least it was something. Then it got stronger and stronger. She started to breathe on her own then."

In the distance, a faint wail of sirens could be heard. Maria stood silently by her husband, watching him as he worked on Mrs. Syberson.

"I wanted to move her onto the lawn, and I got Maria and two other people to help me. It was obvious that Vivian was in very grave condition, so I asked my wife to put in another call to the fire department."

Initially, when Caballero entered the burning building, Maria was upset at him for taking such a risk. As she stood outside and counted the seconds that her husband was inside, any anger she felt evaporated and concern took over. She knew it must be very bad if he was taking so long to come out.

"After I called the ambulance, I went back down to be with Ray. When he brought Vivian out, she was dead. He brought her back. It was then I realized that he was burned badly. I saw something was wrong

with his hair; it was on fire. I told him it was burning and when he went
to put it out, his hair just fell out. The skin was melting off his arms and
chest. There was a burned blanket stuck to his back. Ray thought he just
had burns on his arm. He didn't know how it really was.

"When the ambulance arrived, the paramedics started working on
Vivian. All the adrenaline in Ray's system had kept him from hurting,
but then he started to come down from it and the pain took over. He
started yelling that he was burning. There was a garden hose in the front
yard and I started spraying him. He was screaming in pain. I didn't know
what to do.

"I never thought I would ever see anything like that happen in my life
and certainly not to my husband. While I was spraying Ray, the first fire
department trucks arrived from Engine Companies 7 and 91. They told
me to keep putting water on him and I did."

The paramedics' first concern was Vivian. At that moment, she was
barely clinging to life. Another ambulance arrived and began caring for
Caballero. Chief Bobby Hoff was one of the first firefighters to arrive.
He and Ray knew each other.

"Chief, I don't think I'm going to be able to make it to work today."

Smiling at Ray's gross understatement, he looked at him and said,
"No shit, Caballero."

It was decided that Mrs. Syberson would be sent to the burn center
at Cook County Hospital and Ray would go to the burn center at Loyola University Hospital. It was a twenty-five minute drive. By then, he
was shaking uncontrollably and racked with pain.

"When I rode to the hospital in the ambulance with Ray, I thought
to myself, Well, this will be difficult, but he's my husband and we'll get
through it. I wasn't really scared, not yet.

"They took him right into the emergency room. I waited outside to
speak with the doctor. I knew we were in trouble when a priest wanted
to talk to me.

"He told me that Raymond was in very critical condition and might
not make it. He asked me if there was anyone I wanted to come to the

hospital to see my husband because it might be for the last time. He said he was going to give Ray the last rites. Then he said he wanted to pray with me, and we did.

"I was really frightened. I had never considered Raymond not making it. It didn't occur to me before the priest came out.

"Then the doctors came out and told me that Ray wanted to talk to me. I had to scrub up and get into a sterile gown with a mask. They were very concerned about infection. They told me that he wasn't going to look the same and that I should be prepared to see him very swollen.

"It was a very good thing that I had a mask on. This wasn't the Raymond I had gone to the hospital with. His face was horribly swollen. I couldn't let him know how shocked I was. I knew then I was going to have to be strong for everyone.

"I hung in pretty well until after his first surgery. There isn't any way I was prepared for what I saw when he came out. They had shaved his skin off, the way you would make thin slices of cheese. There were staples everywhere holding pieces of skin that had been grafted from less burned places."

When her husband was out of sight, Maria broke down. She loved him desperately and was so afraid she could lose him. He was in such awful pain and his pain was hers. Standing alone in the hallway at Loyola University Hospital, she cried. All of the fear and hope poured out of her. Maria had reached her limit.

One hundred percent of Raymond Caballero's body was burned; 30 percent of those burns were third degree and 20 to 25 percent were second degree.

"In the days following the surgery, Ray was so down. I just kept telling him not to worry, he was going to be fine. We were going to get through it together. It wasn't really working. He thought of himself as a disfigured man, but I didn't. He was still my Raymond.

"You could see he was thinking about things and wanted to tell me something. I asked him what was wrong and he said to me, 'If you want to take the children and leave me, I will understand. Nobody is going to want to look at me anymore.' It just made me love him more. He will always be my Raymond."

After twenty-two days in the burn unit, Caballero was going crazy from the lack of activity, but he responded to the treatment very well. He had come a long way from the two and three scrubbing procedures daily. As he lay on a steel table while the dead skin was peeled off, he suffered incredible pain, and his body was one massive open wound. He would ask if there was anything he could be given for pain, but they had already given him the maximum dosage. Initially, he was fed through a tube in his nose. The IV solutions had to be given through the femoral artery in his groin because too much damage was done to his arms. The doctors gave strict instructions that he was not to be given a mirror, and all were removed from his hospital room.

The administration of the Chicago Fire Department rallied around Caballero as well. Chief Stanley Spann made it very clear that regardless of his off-duty status at the time of the fire, this was an on-duty injury. "He told me that my family was being taken care of and that I should concentrate on getting better. He was straight with me and it really helped me. I knew I didn't have to worry about Maria and the kids."

Maria was confronted with doing all the chores she and Ray had done together. "When Raymond was burned, I hadn't realized how large our family really was. The Chicago Fire Department lent their emotional and physical support to us daily. The chaplain, Father Thomas Mulcrone, called or visited. It was wonderful. They were there for me and I won't ever forget that."

Caballero was getting stronger every day. The confinement in the hospital was now taking its toll on him. "I told my doctor one day that I had to get out of there. I couldn't see my kids and go outside and play with them. A few days later he came in and said I could go home. They taught Maria how to take care of me, and I got out of there. It went so much faster because they did all of my skin grafts at one time. Normally, this would have been a three-step process, but because I was in top condition, they did it all at one time. It took eight or nine hours."

Nine months later, Raymond Caballero went back to full duty as a Chicago firefighter. A few days after he returned to work, Vivian lost her battle with the flames. An investigation determined the source of the fire was an electric hotplate. Vivian had been using it and slid it under the bed when she was finished. She had neglected to turn it off.

Ray received about thirty awards for his heroic conduct that morning. They included the Lambert Tree Award, which is the city's top medal of valor. The International Association of Fire Chiefs, in conjunction with the Motorola Corporation, bestowed on him their top award, the Benjamin Franklin Fire Service Award for Valor. The Medal of Valor from the Carnegie Foundation was given to him. The top Medal of Valor from *Firehouse* magazine went to him as well. In addition to all the other awards, Raymond Caballero was the International Association of Firefighters Firefighter of the Year for the world.

Looking back on that morning he reflects, "I just ran in there and tried to help. I really wasn't thinking of the consequences of getting hurt or anything like that.

"All in all, it turned out fine, I'm still healthy. I have some scarring on my body, but I think I still look good. Maria and my children, and a lot of other people, are proud of me and that feels wonderful. Not too bad for a Puerto Rican kid from the projects."

No, not bad at all.

6

THE LABYRINTH

December 3, 1999

Worcester, Massachusetts

Paul A. Brotherton, Timothy P. Jackson,
Jeremiah M. Lucey, James F. Lyons, Joseph T.
McGuirk, Thomas E. Spencer

In 1905, the Worcester Cold Storage and Warehouse Company building was constructed at 256 Franklin Street, in the center of Worcester, Massachusetts. Business was good, and seven years later, the building was nearly doubled in size to become a 94,176-square-foot, six-story maze. By 1991, the boom times were gone, and the building was boarded up. After that time, homeless people claimed residence in the structure.

On December 3, 1999, at 6:13 P.M., an off-duty police officer saw smoke rising from the derelict cold storage building, and Box 1438 alarm was struck at the corner of Franklin and Arctic Streets—sending out four engines, two ladder companies, and one rescue company. Three minutes later, the first unit arrived at the corner and saw smoke showing from the building.

Six Worcester, Massachusetts, firefighters were killed in this blaze.
Clockwise from top left: Paul A. Brotherton, Timothy P. Jackson,
Thomas E. Spencer, James F. Lyons, Jeremiah M. Lucey, Joseph T. McGuirk.

That evening, Worcester District Fire Chief Michael McNamee was making his evening rounds, stopping at various stations to pick up administrative paperwork. He was in his car when Box 1438 was struck. His first response was to shake his head and think, That's a bad building.

Driving on Interstate 290, the elevated expressway that works its way through downtown Worcester, the chief could see the old landmark, which sat only thirty feet from the highway. A small amount of smoke was rising from the building. As he arrived, he struck the second alarm as a precautionary measure.

The first order of business was to determine where the fire was in the building. Two aerial ladders, with the ability to reach one hundred feet in the air, were at the scene. Firefighters were dispatched from the ladder trucks to check the roof. One crew went up on a ladder and the other used an interior stairway. On the roof, they vented the elevator shaft to allow the billowing smoke an escape path.

Several stairwells were inside the building, but only one of them went from the first floor directly to the roof. Because the building had been constructed in more than one phase, the stairway system had no continuity. The interior covering on the eighteen-inch-thick brick walls was asphalt-impregnated cork between six and eighteen inches, four inches of polystyrene and polyurethane, and a thin layer of glassboard.

Chief McNamee was inside the building supervising the interior attack on the fire. At 6:22, the fire was discovered in the area next to the elevator shaft on the second floor. The roof venting was working, which kept the smoke and heat at a minimum. Five two-and-a-half-inch hoses were inside the building by that time, which would give an ample supply of water to fight the fire.

When the second alarm sounded, the deputy chief of the department responded. After he arrived, District Chief McNamee became the interior incident commander. He walked up to the third floor to see if there was any extension of the fire. Crews were already searching the area when he got there.

A call came in from a sandwich shop owner across the street from the building. He said he knew that homeless people were living in the building. "We would have searched anyway, but with that information, we did a walk-through," McNamee remembered.

Standing on the third floor, McNamee looked into the light, smoky haze. "It was dark outside by now, not that it mattered. Inside there it is always night. The only sound you could hear was the fire. We were so isolated from the outside world.

"While the crews worked, I thought I would take a walk around on the third floor. I had been standing in the stairwell initially, but now I went through a couple of doors. I went on the other side of the firewall from when the building was expanded. The fire hadn't extended itself, and that was encouraging.

"I went into one particular room and when I started to leave, I didn't know which door I had come in through. All the doors looked alike. I tried one, that didn't look right, then another, then another. I was starting to worry by now. I stopped and listened for a minute or so, and I heard noises coming from the far side of the room. I was completely turned around. The noises were guys humping equipment up the stairs. I was able to home in on the noise and work my way out. That's the kind of building it was, you could turn around and be lost.

"What we didn't know when we arrived was the fire had about a sixty-minute head start on us. It had been started by a homeless couple who had used a candle for light. They had an argument that turned physical. One of them fell into the candle, tipping it over. It was a small fire, but rather than report it, they fled."

Several teams of firefighters were above the third floor searching for the homeless people who had already left. Chief McNamee was back in the stairwell. As the interior incident commander, he intended to direct the firefighting operation from the stairwell because that location gave him the best read on the progress of the fire.

"I decided to go up and take a look at the floor above me. There was almost no smoke at my location. I was concerned that the complexity of the rooms and the stairwell setup might not have given me the true read on the fire, although there were no reports from any of the firefighters on the upper floors.

"I walked up one floor and took a look at conditions. Halfway up to the fourth floor, it went from barely any smoke to zero visibility in five seconds. I issued an order to clear the upper floors. At that point, all I wanted was to get everybody down and do a head count and then continue to fight the fire for a little bit and see what happened. Deputy Chief John Fenton called for a third alarm to be struck.

"I knew there was a heavy rescue team [the most sophisticated level of rescue units] above me. That unit consisted of six firefighters and a fire officer. They broke into two teams and conducted a rescue search to inspect the area for fire extension as well as look for the homeless people. My main concern at that point was to pull all my firefighters down from the upper floors and go into a defensive mode. I no longer thought we were in a position to attack the fire; it had gotten away from us. We were going to back out and reassess our options.

"In my position, I knew I had the best spot to see the teams when they came down. It was possible they could go off the roof or down another staircase, but since this was the stairway that led directly to the outside, it gave me the best chance to see everyone when they came down."

The fire officer from Rescue 1 came down and met with Chief McNamee.

"Chief, I know Paul Brotherton and Jerry Lucey are searching the floor above me. Keep an eye out for them."

McNamee said he would, and the fire officer continued down to the rescue truck to do a head count. The chief waited at the stairwell, watching above for the two firefighters. They didn't come down. Neither firefighter was found at the truck.

"The fire officer came back to me and asked again if I had seen them. I said I hadn't. Then almost immediately, we heard from Brotherton and Lucey. It wasn't good."

"Rescue to Command, I need help on the floor below the top floor of the building. We are lost. Rescue to Command, we need help on the fourth floor."

It was now 6:49. Central dispatch cleared the radio channel for emergency traffic only. Within a few seconds, the lost firefighters radioed again.

"We have an emergency, Command. We are two floors down from the roof. This is the rescue company. Come now, two floors down from the roof. Guys, not the top floor, one floor down."

A brief period of time went by and contact was made with Brotherton and Lucey again to find out their status. Chief McNamee wanted to commence a search for them immediately. He hoped they would be able to give some landmark to aid in their being located.

"We need air. We need air. I'm sharing a tank off me right now. We are lost. You've got to send a rescue team up here for us. Second floor down from the roof, two floors down. We were on the roof, and then we checked the next floor down. Now we are on the next one. Hurry."

Chief McNamee ran outside to look at the building to determine how many floors the cold storage building had. It was very difficult to assess, as there were only a few windows on the lower floors. He was still unsure, but put it at either five or six. They had said the fourth, but if there were only five floors, that could mean they were really on the third.

Engine 3 and Ladder 2 had arrived from headquarters station as part of the third alarm and were standing by for assignment. James Lyons and Joseph McGuirk rode on Engine 3. The officer in charge of the ladder truck was Lieutenant Thomas Spencer and one of his firefighters was Timothy Jackson.

The Worcester Cold Storage and Warehouse was in the shape of an L when viewed from the air. Brotherton and Lucey were lost and in the worst possible spot to effect a rescue. They were in the tip of the L and far away from the stairwell that could lead to safety, either by going down or to the roof. In addition, their search for any homeless people had been fruitless.

"Since we couldn't say for sure which floor they were on, we had to search the third, fourth, and fifth. I didn't want to take any chances and miss them. I made it clear that the searchers were to come out immediately if their low-air alarms sounded.

"When the alarm goes off they would only have a few minutes of air left and I wanted them to come out and get a fresh air bottle. With the way the building was laid out, and with the thickness of the smoke, it was not an environment to try and make it without air."

A search rope is used by firefighters when they head into an area that is difficult to see in or has a complicated layout. The rope is tied off to a stationary object and then is fed out by the firefighter as he or she advances. If he becomes disoriented he simply follows the rope back to where it is tied off.

"Ladder 2 was one of the crews that went up to do the search. Tom Spencer and Timmy Jackson were in that crew. Half of their crew stopped to clear out plywood from some of the windows in the stairwell. The idea was to get some ventilation on the stairs to keep the smoke out of there as much as possible. It was still zero visibility by the time you got to the second floor."

Chief McNamee looked at Spencer's face as he passed within inches of him heading up the stairs. The look in his eyes was a "come on let's get this thing done" kind of look.

A crew from Ladder 1 was up on the roof when the emergency call came out from Brotherton and Lucey. Captain Michael Coakley and Bert Davis came down two floors to search for the two missing firefighters. They put on their SCBAs and walked into the poisonous black cloud that inhabited the building. When they got to the second floor down, they started their search where Brotherton and Lucey said they were.

Heading off the stairs, they made their way in. The men were in a series of freezers. All of the doors had flush hardware on the inside. When a door was closed, it was very hard to find the latch to open it. With the heavy gloves the firefighters wore and without a door handle to grab, the smooth latch just felt like part of the wall—and given the smoke conditions, it wasn't possible to use a flashlight with much effectiveness. The firefighters went into one room and started doing a right-hand search. They went around the room in a counterclockwise manner. One wall was searched, then two, three, four, all with no results.

In addition to no results, they had no door to get out. Again, they checked and could find no way out. They were trapped. The captain said to himself, "We're going to die in here. Not only am I going to die, but I'm going to kill one of my guys in the process too." Then suddenly, and without explanation, the apparently invisible door popped open just a bit. There was no plausible explanation for the door doing that, it just did.

As they backtracked out to find the stairwell, Captain Coakley's air ran out and he was forced to take off his mask. He ran down four flights of stairs in the smoke. When he passed Chief McNamee, he could barely breathe. He got outside, changed air tanks, and went right back in to continue the search. The ambulance crew wanted to transport him, but he would have none of it. Coakley stayed until the end.

"We called to Paul and Jerry and told them to activate their PASS [personal alert safety system] alarms. The shrill sound of the alarm would help us find them. They told us they had done it already. The men on the floors above could hear nothing. We had everyone stop talking on the radios and those on the upper floors listened, but could hear nothing."

The men from Engine 3 stood on the stairs at the fifth-floor level and stopped breathing so they could hear the PASS alarms. They heard nothing.

Lieutenant Spencer and Jackson were on the fifth floor searching. They told command they had joined up with men from Engine 3, Lyons and McGuirk. A few minutes later, they asked by radio if the missing firefighters had been found. The answer was no.

Chief McNamee remained at his position, commanding the interior search and fire attack. "We were rotating men in and out. We had not found the missing firefighters, but we were searching. A little after seven o'clock, one of the firefighters from Ladder 2 radioed Lieutenant Spencer from the first floor of the building, asking what the lieutenant's position was."

Lieutenant Spencer responded, "We came up the stairwell. We are on the fifth floor."

"What is your position on the fifth floor?" asked the firefighter.

"Good question."

"Repeat please."

"We are doing a sweep. I believe we are in the front of the building."

A few minutes passed before Lieutenant Spencer made another radio transmission to Command. "Chief, get a company up the stairwell to the fifth floor. We can't locate the stairwell. Or give us a sign as to which way to go. We are running low on air and we want to get out of here."

Four minutes later, at 7:14, the lieutenant radioed again. "Send someone up to the stairwell to the fifth floor and stand in the doorway and start yelling. We can't find the door."

Firefighters immediately headed into the abyss. On the fifth floor, they called and called. They lifted their facepieces and yelled, but there was no response. The insulation in the building sucked in the sound.

Human chains were used for some of the searching on the upper floors. The firefighters were lying on their stomachs, head to foot, moving ahead looking for the lost men. Each time nothing was found or heard.

At 7:24, another head count was done. Six firefighters were now missing in the cold storage building. Word reached Chief McNamee that heat on the stairway just below the fifth floor was so intense they were unable to make the floor. Seven minutes later, a call was made to the men from Ladder 2 and Engine 3. They didn't answer, but they had never put out a Mayday. Six minutes later, the same call was made with no answer. Another call went out at 7:48. Again there was no response.

A few minutes before eight o'clock, Lieutenant Jim Pijus, who had been on the upper floors with the other firefighters, told Chief McNamee they had been driven from the third floor. Word also came that the structural integrity of the building appeared compromised at the fourth floor.

A thermal imaging unit was brought into the building to begin a high-tech search for the missing firefighters. This would allow the searching firefighters to see a warm body through the thick smoke. In three minutes, the unit failed because of the extreme heat.

"I stood at the doorway leading to the stairs," McNamee remembers. "After talking with Lieutenant Pijus, I knew it was over. If he couldn't make the third floor, no one could. In my heart, I knew six men were dead. My friends were gone.

"There were about a dozen or so firefighters ready to go into the breach. They had fear in their faces, but it was a determined kind. If I let them go by me, they were dead too. I stretched my arms out to touch the doorjamb on both sides.

"No more! It's over!"

One firefighter called out in disbelief, "What do you mean, Chief?"

Another yelled, "We have people in there. What do you mean, we're not going back up?"

"They're gone. Now let's go outside and set up for a defensive fire."

In an instant, any confrontation was over. The firefighters' heads dropped and their arms hung loose at their sides. They went from defiant to downcast. Their feet shuffled as they left the building.

The last man out was Michael McNamee. Left behind were the dead firefighters Paul Brotherton, Timothy Jackson, Jeremiah Lucey, James Lyons, Joseph McGuirk, and Lieutenant Thomas Spencer. Two lost their lives trying to rescue homeless people, and the others died trying to rescue their brothers.

Four months later, forty-seven-year-old Captain Michael Coakley retired, another casualty of the Worcester Cold Storage and Warehouse. Coakley, who was an athlete and had never smoked, had only 30 percent lung capacity.

Years before, Michael and Joanne McNamee had bought a house in Worcester. A little boy from across the street marveled at his neighbor's stories of firefighting. The little boy grew up to follow that same path. In the early morning hours of December 4, 1999, Chief McNamee slowly walked up the sidewalk to the home of that little boy from across the street.

James Lyons's mother, Joan, came to the door and stared into the heartbroken eyes of the chief. "Michael, do you have bad news for me?"

McNamee remembered thinking, "She never called me Michael before then, just Mike." The chief's visit was the first of two that night. District chief Randy Chavoor would deliver the heartbreaking news to four other families.

It would be eight days before the last man, Paul Brotherton, was recovered from the collapsed building. The search was done by the same men and women who had fought side by side with their fallen comrades. They were determined to leave no trace of their friends behind. From the wreckage, Timothy Jackson's wedding ring was retrieved. It is now suspended from a gold chain around his widow's neck.

All six firefighters received the Medal of Valor. In honor of the extraordinary effort of the men and women of the Worcester Fire Department who worked the fire, all were granted a unit citation.

Christmas came and went that month. Fifteen children lost their fathers, five wives their husbands, and the Lyons family lost their son. For those connected with that awful night, nothing would ever be the same.

7

SEVENTY FEET TO DAYLIGHT

August 9, 1994

Los Angeles County Fire Department

Larry Collins and Collin "Corky" Cook

Urban Search and Rescue Unit One (USAR-1) of the Los Angeles County Fire Department was training with the U.S. Coast Guard and the Los Angeles County Life Guard Division off Redondo Beach in Southern California. They were practicing having a Coast Guard helicopter pluck firefighters out of the water in preparation for potential marine disasters.

More than fifty miles away in Newhall, Jaime (pronounced HY-mae) Garcia was inspecting shafts that had been drilled into the soil. The thirty-inch-diameter shafts were almost seventy feet deep and were to receive a steel reinforcement cage and then concrete after Jaime approved them. A powerful earthquake had destroyed two homes at the location. The concrete-filled shafts were meant to join the new foundations with the bedrock, and Jaime had already inspected several of them. Nearby,

Collin Cook is being raised out of the seventy-foot-deep hole with Jaime Garcia hanging unconscious below him. Larry Collins can be seen in the center of the picture (fourth from left) without a helmet.

one of the workers watched the inspector carefully pull the plywood cover off another hole. Then incredibly, Jaime Garcia disappeared.

Captain Larry Collins and his USAR-1 rescue crew got the call at 10:40 A.M. "Man trapped in a shaft." Collins requested a Los Angeles County Fire Department Bell 412 rescue helicopter to respond to the pier at Redondo Beach to pick them up. When this unit was formed, Fire Chief Michael Freeman assigned them to the heliport facility because he wanted them to have the ultimate in mobility. This was exactly the kind of situation the chief had envisioned.

USAR-1's rescue truck was parked at the Redondo Beach location. When they left their station for the drill, the team members had taken every piece of equipment they owned on the truck. The rescue truck was, in essence, a fire truck with no hoses and was what Captain Collins described as a giant toolbox on wheels. Back on the shore, the team unloaded several items they would need for the deep-shaft rescue.

Firefighter Specialist Michael Layhee was also on the crew. Normally, he drove the truck, but because of his expertise in technical rescue operations, Collins wanted Layhee with him in the helicopter. The two men had a special bond that was linked by a long history together. If this was going to be another incredibly dangerous mission, Collins knew he needed Layhee with him. Another member of the crew drove the truck to the rescue site while the other two flew in the helicopter.

Additional fire units were on the way to the rescue site as well, including Hazmat Task Force 76, the hazardous materials unit, which had equipment that could supply clean air into the shaft.

Truck 73 from the Santa Colina station also responded. Firefighter Specialist Collin Cook, known as "Corky," was on that truck, and he was one of the original USAR members. He arrived at the construction site a short time before Collins and Layhee.

As he approached the hole, Cook saw L.A. County Firefighter Paramedic Kelly Lynn lying on his stomach, talking seven stories down to Garcia. The area around the hole was now covered with pieces of plywood, making a safe platform to communicate. To make doubly sure no one else fell in, a wooden ladder from Engine 124 was placed over the hole.

Jaime was afraid the firefighters would look at the impossible task before them and just leave, but his rescuers repeatedly assured him that they would not leave without him. Cook and Lynn just wanted him to hang on until someone could get down to him. Jaime was critically injured, and all he could see from where he lay was a dime-sized button of sky.

Acting as captain for 73, Cook immediately rigged two twenty-foot ladders together into an A frame, onto which they would affix a pulley system to raise and lower the rescuer and extract the victim.

The helicopter landed, and out came Collins and Layhee. They approached the hole and lay on their stomachs, using a powerful light to peer into the black pit.

"I took that light and looked down trying to see Jaime," Collins said. "It was a futile effort. The dirt just absorbed the light. You couldn't see anything past fifty feet or so. We talked to him, and he said he was badly hurt. But as long as he was able to speak, we stayed encouraged. All the way there, I kept thinking about Layhee and his wife and kids. He had a lot to lose and I didn't. I asked him if he wanted me to go down first. I just felt it was best to send the person with the least to lose and that was me. He would have none of it and said, 'Nope, I'll go.' Layhee reminded me of prior rescues when I was the first man down, and that now it was his turn.

"I knew that Layhee was a bit apprehensive about going in, but we had been in some tight spots before. We had already been in all kinds of rescues together, and some were pretty crazy. We had a good plan and it wasn't too much different than if we were going to snag somebody off a cliff. But we both knew that if there was a collapse, it was going to be a bad, bad situation."

Whoever stayed on top was in charge of the rescue. Collins was the captain, but rank didn't really matter at that point. Layhee suited up and wore a mask with an attached air hose with a two-way communication system built in. He was lowered into the hole feetfirst, carrying a victim harness with him. Maintaining communication between the rescuer and the director of the operation would be critical.

"When I got down about forty-five or fifty feet or so, the shaft began to narrow and it was obvious that I couldn't do it," recounted Layhee. "I was too broad in the shoulders for the size of the hole. I could see Jaime, and it looked like he was buried in dirt. I was concerned about getting stuck and having to be rescued myself. That would take up time that could be spent on the victim. Even if I did get to the bottom, I wouldn't be able to move around and make a rescue.

"They pulled me up, and Collins already had his rescue harness on. We talked for a moment, and I told him what I had seen in the hole and what I thought he should take with him. We reversed roles. He went down and I was in charge."

While Layhee was in the hole, Collins had gone through a series of backup plans. "I talked to the incident commander, who was a battalion chief, on the scene and we discussed different scenarios. Plan A was already underway, but we needed more than one alternative approach. I wanted another plan in case there was a collapse or if Mike couldn't free Jaime.

"I got some of the engineers who were involved in the Metro Rail project assigned to the rescue site. These guys were experts in tunneling. Plan B was going to involve boring a secondary shaft from the side. I was able to get some of that machinery dispatched to us.

"Plan C was to use an air knife with a vacuum system. The knife works off of compressed air, and it cuts through compacted earth very quickly. The vacuum sucks all the loose dirt to the surface. We carried one on the rescue truck, so acquiring one wouldn't pose any problem.

"With the work Corky, Joe Correa, and the other guys from 73 had done prior to our arrival, I felt good about the way we were heading. Then came word from Mike that he was too big to go any farther. I knew it was my turn. I am a lot smaller than he, and I was confident I could make it to the bottom."

As he considered various rescue options, Captain Collins worried about an aftershock or something that would cause a collapse. A few months earlier they had a severe earthquake, and the ground still shook with some regularity. "By then one of the Metro Rail engineers had arrived, and I asked him how the shaft looked. He said it looked good.

"Layhee checked my harness, and everything looked OK. There I was, over the top of the hole and looking down and I couldn't see a thing. I checked my radio communications with him, and looked into the hole again. I still could see nothing.

"It was show time, and we had to get on with it. They started lowering me down. A lantern was on my helmet, and as I was going down, I felt like the main character in *2001: A Space Odyssey* as he went through the wormhole. I could see the layers of dirt going past me. Then I could see Jaime. Above me the sky looked so distant, and I knew just how deep I was. I didn't look up anymore; it was better for me to just concentrate on what was down there." It took less than two minutes to lower Collins to the bottom of the shaft. He had them stop him just above the inspector. Collins began his assessment of the situation.

"It looked to me like he was buried up to his chest in dirt. If that was the case, it was going to take six to eight hours just to dig him out. I didn't know it then, but Jaime had fallen with such force he drove his knees up to his chest and severed his spinal cord. He had also fractured his pelvis and broken both legs. In addition, six ribs were broken, resulting in both his lungs and spleen being ruptured. He also had a lacerated liver. After all that, he was still alive and able to talk."

Collins was now only a few feet above Jaime. Looking up at the man who had come to rescue him, Jaime spoke. "My back is broken."

"How do you know?"

"I can feel it's broken."

Collins shared this information with Layhee. "Lower me very slowly, just an inch or two at a time."

Finally, Collins touched down with one foot on each side of Jaime. In addition to being an expert rescue firefighter, he is a paramedic. He began to check the back of a man who only two hours before had been simply doing his job, and was now fighting for his life. Without sharing his thoughts, the captain made a preliminary diagnosis. "I thought at the very least he would be a paraplegic."

Jaime had few illusions about his prospects. His speech was labored as the two men spoke. "I don't think I'm going to make it out of here."

Collins wanted to make sure Jaime understood the Los Angeles County Fire Department was in this for the long haul. "No, that isn't so. We are going to get you out of here. It might take a while because I have to figure out a couple of things, but we're going to get you out of here and we're not leaving until we take you out."

The dispirited Jaime was not immediately assured. "I'll never see daylight again."

"Someone is going to stay with you the whole time. We are not going to abandon you. Jaime, you are coming out with us."

This seemed to boost his spirits, but he was in severe pain. Collins knelt with his legs wedged against the walls as he attempted to free the inspector. Nothing worked.

"Normally, we would worry about his spinal condition and stabilize his back, but this was different. I reached down between my legs and tried to free him. My plan was to pull him up, but with his knees wedged up to his chest, somehow his legs had to swing under his body. I tried to dig around him, but it was like concrete. They were supposed to drill into bedrock and they had.

"I tried to lift him, but each time he started screaming. I was pulling him right at the spot where he had all the broken ribs. If I pulled too hard, I would separate his spinal column. I worked quarter-inch by quarter-inch to get a strap underneath his legs. My thinking was to lift him just as he was.

"I was breathing hard and I couldn't do it. It was hot down there and I was probably suffering the first stages of heat exhaustion. I realized that I couldn't succeed because I didn't have the reach. I knew what I had to do—invert myself. I told Mike to raise me up. I disconnected myself from part of my safety harness and scrunched myself up in a ball and flipped upside down.

"Jaime looked up at me and said, 'You're not going to get me out of here, it's not working.' I told him that we were going to get him out, but that it was taking time to figure out the way to do it. I didn't want to hurt him. I didn't tell him, or Layhee up top, but I was really fighting nausea by then.

"I had been down there for forty or forty-five minutes, and Layhee continually asked me how I was doing. I kept telling him that I was doing fine. I had to get Jaime to a standing position. It would have been good to have a second set of eyes down there with me to get another perspective. By then it was very apparent that Jaime was in very serious medical condition, and if I didn't get him out of there, he wouldn't make it.

"I was using my neck as a fulcrum, pressing my head against the wall to control my body while I was hanging upside down. You hear about people operating on adrenaline, and that was the case for me. I wasn't aware of it at the time, but I was ripping the muscles in my back and neck with every pull."

Layhee listened intently to every transmission by Collins. By now, he had been down in the hole for more than an hour and was starting to sound fatigued. Layhee had heard enough and told his captain, "We're pulling you out." They waited until Collins turned himself around and assured Jaime that someone else would be right down.

Jaime was starting to drift in and out of consciousness. As Collins started to make his way to the surface, the inspector spoke to him. "Tell my fiancée that I love her, because I don't know if I'm going to get out of here."

"OK, but another firefighter is coming right down to take my place, so keep breathing."

The whole time Collins was down the hole, Captains Joseph Correa and Mike Short manned the ropes. They were following the direction of Layhee, who received his instructions from Collins. This is a typical situation during rescues. Everyone remembers who goes in the hole, but the rescue can't happen without firefighters like Correa and Short.

As Collins was pulled back to safety, he watched Jaime. "As I was being pulled up and out, I had the distinct feeling of an angel or a bird as I rose above Jaime's body and watched him become smaller and smaller. As I looked back in sadness at him, I couldn't see him at all. It was disturbing to me, knowing I was leaving a victim all alone, like I was abandoning him, even though someone else would be down there in a moment.

"It must have been a very lonely feeling for him. Not knowing if he would ever see his family again. All the pain and agony he felt and then asking me to talk to his fiancée because he didn't think he would get out. I didn't feel like a success as I went up."

As time passed on the surface, Cook realized he would be going into the hole. For a while he didn't know if he'd be going to rescue Collins, Jaime, or both. For now, Collins was being extricated, and the only task at hand was the rescue of this broken man. As he waited to be lowered, Cook made sure his harness was properly fastened, and he mentally prepared himself.

When Collins reached the surface, Layhee saw that the captain was in rough shape. "He was really fatigued and his neck was hurting him. I should have pulled him out of there sooner." Collins had to be transported to the hospital by ambulance. His maneuverings in the hole resulted in severe damage to the muscles in his back and neck.

"I am pretty claustrophobic," Cook explained. "I thought it was going to be a challenge for me to try and get through that. I was thinking mostly about the soil in the area and my gear. While Larry was down there, I talked a lot with Mike Layhee and knew what was going on. It helped me a lot when it became necessary to go in because I didn't have to spend a lot of time preparing myself."

Cook clipped two more lights on his harness and arranged to have a light lowered with him. At the last minute, he shoved a small gardening shovel into his belt.

"I heard a lot of radio traffic when Collins was in the hole. I asked Mike Layhee if he could handle everything on the radio unless it was super-important for me to talk. I just wanted to concentrate on Jaime.

"I still wanted more assurance about the soil conditions. I asked one of the engineers at the site what he thought. He told me the soil conditions were good and a collapse wasn't likely. I said to him, 'OK, let's say I put the harness on you and you're going down. What do you think?' He said, 'I think if I were you, I'd do it.' He went on to explain to me what to look for in the way of problem soil conditions. I felt better about it. Then I talked to Larry for a moment and knew more or less what to expect when I got down there."

When the rescue squad first responded to the call, a paramedic was already at the scene. Kelly Lynn had been lying on his stomach and talking with Jaime when the others arrived. When Collins was extricated, another firefighter paramedic, Steve Olson, took over and kept talking to Jaime, assuring him no one was giving up. Cook talked with the paramedic and got a sense of the mental state Jaime was in.

"Then it was time to go down. As my face passed the surface of the ground, I thought of my wife and my kids and how important they were to me. In my firefighting career, whenever I have faced great danger, they have been on my mind—big time. As I was being lowered, I looked at the soil. It must have been me, but I kept seeing the things the soil engineer had told me to watch for as far as dangerous soil conditions.

"All the time I was on my way down, I talked to Jaime. He didn't really respond too much. When I got to him, I told him I was there to help him out."

Things were not going well for Jaime, who had slipped into unconsciousness. However, this allowed Cook to move him without inflicting a great amount of pain.

"When he stopped breathing and went unconscious, I was thinking it was a full-arrest situation. I tried to get a pulse and I could feel a faint one when I first got down there, but then I couldn't detect any respiration. This guy had fallen almost seventy feet to a rock floor, and he was in bad shape.

"I never did look up while I was being lowered down. When I was down there, I knew if I looked up I wouldn't see any comforting sights like daylight, so I didn't. I just focused on what I had to do. Actually, when I was being lowered, I told them at one point to speed up. I just wanted to get down there and get to work."

Knowing that the time had come to extricate Jaime or face losing him at the bottom of the seventy-foot hole, Cook placed a harness around Jaime and hooked it to himself. "I told them to get me to the surface in a hurry. At that point, the only thing I was worried about was getting Jaime out of the hole and to the hospital." As he had done on the way down, he requested that they speed it up.

Back at the surface, all the attention focused upon Jaime. The paramedic team performed only a basic amount of work on him at the scene, and then he was off to the hospital.

Layhee was worried that with all the movement around the hole, somebody might fall in again. He yelled repeated warnings to keep clear of the hole. As soon as he could, Layhee had it completely covered with plywood.

Two days later, Jaime Garcia died. He never regained consciousness.

Larry Collins and Collin "Corky" Cook received the Medal of Valor from the Los Angeles County Fire Department. They were also awarded the Medal of Valor from the California State Fireman's Association. In addition, they received a Medal for Valor from *Firehouse* magazine as part of their Heroism and Community Service program.

Looking back on the awards, Cook reflected, "It was a great honor to get the awards, but I have mixed emotions about it. We got the medals, but Jaime lost his life."

Larry Collins concurred, saying, "When you report for duty you're not thinking about awards or recognition. You want to do your job to the best of your ability and you are willing to make certain sacrifices and take certain risks. That is how it was that day, only we fell short of our objective because Jaime died."

8

DADDY'S ANGEL

September 30, 1998

Los Angeles, California

Timothy Wuerfel Jr.

It was a defining moment for several of those who answered the late afternoon call to 230 East 73rd Street on September 30, 1998. Task Force 33 was dispatched to the house along with Rescue 833.

Firefighters Silas Clarke and Steven Lopez were working the rescue ambulance that day. Lopez raced the ambulance to the house fire and pulled up to find nothing. No flames, no commotion. But a cloud of thick, black smoke was rising in the sky, indicating that the fire was actually on the next street over. They had been dispatched to the wrong address.

"I made the decision to leave the ambulance on 74th Street and for us to walk over to where we saw the smoke," remembers Lopez. "Silas and I went down between the houses and hopped fences so we could get to the fire quicker.

Timothy Wuerfel Jr. (on right), Los Angeles Fire Department.

"We jumped over the last fence and ran to the burning house. There were three or four men trying to hammer a hole in the stucco wall so we could enter the house that way. As we got closer to the men, Silas heard a little girl's cry for help coming from inside the house through a window. We knew we had to get inside the house that second."

"When the hole was big enough to crawl through, I went in," recounts Clarke. "I didn't last long, though, because the smoke was banked down to the floor. It was a thick, black smoke that suffocates. Sometimes you can breathe through the smoke, but not that stuff."

Acting as a team, Clarke came out and Lopez went in. Both firefighters wore full turnout gear, but because they were assigned to a rescue ambulance, they did not have their SCBAs on. With the size of the fire and the amount of smoke, it was clear that the little girl could not last much longer.

"After Silas came out, I went in," explains Lopez. "I was on my hands and knees, feeling as I went along. The smoke blinded me, and I couldn't see anything, just black. I entered a bathroom and checked the perimeter quickly. I kept the wall to my left so I would be able to make my way back out without becoming disoriented. Silas stayed at the entrance and kept in contact with me while I was inside to make sure I was all right and could find my way out if I got lost. Fire was making its way into the bedroom.

"I had to get out. I couldn't get any good air to breathe, and I couldn't hold my breath any longer. When I came out, Tim Wuerfel was there." This was his first day back at work following two weeks off. Wuerfel and his wife, Kimber, had just lost a baby girl. She had miscarried seven and a half months into the pregnancy.

Wuerfel was the inside man assigned to a truck on Task Force 33, which meant he was responsible for opening the front of the structure so firefighters with hoses could make an entrance.

"After I found the front door open, I went around back to establish a second entrance point, and when I got there I heard a voice coming from inside the house. When Steve came back out, I asked him if there was somebody inside. He said, 'Yes, a little girl.'"

Wuerfel secured his SCBA facepiece and prepared to crawl into the burning house. After two weeks of his own grief, he would now do everything he could to prevent more sorrow and tragedy by saving someone else's daughter. Up until this point, Lopez and Clarke had tried to no avail. The little girl's last chance rested on Wuerfel's shoulders. He pulled Lopez near and gave him some last-minute instructions. "Steve, tell the captain that we have a little girl in there, and that I am going in. Then I want you to stay by the hole until I come out. Don't leave."

As Wuerfel disappeared into the opening, Lopez was very nervous. "I was afraid for him because all you could see was fire and smoke."

Wuerfel was now inside. "When I crawled into the house, I first entered a closet that was engulfed by fire. The clothes on the hangers were burning as well as everything on the floor. The smoke was almost to the floor and I couldn't see my hand in front of my face. I didn't know it then, but this closet was where the fire had originated and had already burned through the ceiling and was in the attic.

"I was sweeping my hands back and forth in front of me as I went. There was so much smoke, I could hardly see the flames, but they were there all the while. A lot of times they were just a hazy glow. The flashlight attached to my helmet didn't do any good either. I couldn't see a thing.

"Pretty soon, I was in a bathroom. I could feel the shower enclosure, then the tub, and finally the toilet. There was no little girl. As I went, I called to her over and over again, but she had fallen silent.

"I've been in a room when a flashover occurred. I knew the rest of the crew would be ventilating the roof and would start putting water on the fire, which would lower the temperature. This would diminish the chance for such an event, but crawling on the floor reminded me of the previous flashover I'd been in, which occurred when the carpet burst into flames. I knew I didn't want to experience that again.

"Next, I went back through the closet (which joined the two rooms) and into a bedroom. The bed was burning and so was the furniture. Parts of the carpet were in flames, and I just tried to stay out of them the best I could. There was a lot of heat in there, but I endured it long enough to search the whole room.

"It didn't look good. I was sure she was on that side of the house because that is where I last heard her and so had the others. I knew I wasn't leaving without her, no matter what it took. I knew that Steve and Silas were out there, and if things went bad, they would be there for me.

"Then something happened that I can't explain. I had this feeling that I needed to go back to the bathroom, even though I had already been in there. So back through the burning closet I went."

Outside, Lopez was at the hole in the wall, calling over and over again to Wuerfel to let him know where the opening was. Clarke had run back to the engine to pull an inch-and-three-quarter line back. In his haste, he fell and severely injured his leg, but continued back with the hose. Wuerfel entered the bathroom again, doing the same search; and just as before, visibility was nearly zero. Then he felt something he hadn't during his first search.

"As I skimmed my hands along the floor, I touched her. I was already on my hands and knees, and I bent closer to her for a look. It turned out to be the six-year-old Tammi Smith. Looking into her unconscious face, all covered with soot and saliva, it hit me: she was just like the little girl I lost."

Gathering up the little girl, Wuerfel headed for the hole and freedom. When he emerged, Lopez was waiting to take the unconscious fire victim. "Steve was all set, but I couldn't let her go. I held her so tight as I ran to the front of the house and placed her on the lawn."

Finally, it was Lopez's turn to take over. Lopez bent down and inspected Tammi. "She wasn't breathing enough on her own—only three or four times a minute. I cleared her airway and began mouth-to-mouth resuscitation. In a couple of minutes, she began to breathe on her own, and she was transported to the University of Southern California Medical Center."

Dr. Mark Eckstein said the levels of carbon monoxide were so high that she only had a few minutes left to live when Wuerfel found her. An investigation revealed that she had been playing with matches and started the fire in the closet while her grandmother was in the front of the house.

Within a few days, Wuerfel and Kimber paid a visit to the hospital with a stuffed Dalmatian. Tammi made a complete recovery. The real gift she had been given was a full life ahead of her.

For his actions, Timothy Wuerfel was awarded the Los Angeles Fire Department Medal of Valor. Silas Clarke and Steve Lopez received their department's Award of Merit.

"There had to be a reason I went back to work and went on that call," Wuerfel reflects. "I don't know why I went back to that room again. Maybe I got some help." For Kimber, the rescue made perfect sense. "I believe our little angel guided Tim back to that bathroom to save someone else's little angel."

9

BURNS TO THE HANDS BUT NOT TO THE HEART

July 24, 1998

New York, New York

John "Captain Jack" Pritchard

Captain John Pritchard (also known as "Captain Jack"), one of New York City's most highly decorated firefighters, was running the evening drill for Engine 255 in Brooklyn. The engine company had a reputation in the fire department, the kind they were proud to have. The saying at the house was that you were either on the engine or under it. They were known for very quick turnouts. They drilled twice a day, not to mention all the on-the-job training they got fighting actual fires in Brooklyn. Most days, they wore their bunker (turnout) pants all day long so that they wasted no time putting them on when a call came in. And they came often.

That year, Engine 255 left the station on calls for fires almost four thousand times. On average, they fought more than one structural fire a

John "Captain Jack" Pritchard, FDNY.

day and went to someone in need of medical aid almost four times each day. They were used to working and loved it.

At about eleven o'clock in the evening, during one of 255's drills, a trouble alarm rang for a structure fire about ten blocks away from the firehouse, at 600 East 21st Street, which was the apartment home of ten-month-old Shadae Brophete and her family.

If you count the seconds from when a call comes in to when the firefighters leave the station, you don't have to count high where 255 is concerned. This night was no different. In less than three minutes, the engine was in front of the apartment house, and the captain was giving instructions to his crew. The drill on laying hose at a multistory dwelling had moved locations and was no longer hypothetical. Captain Pritchard broadcast a 10-75, the signal at the FDNY for a working fire.

"People were in the street, waving us down as we pulled up. One of them was a mother who said her little girl was trapped upstairs in the fire. She was screaming that she couldn't get back in to get her," remembers Captain Pritchard.

"I tried to calm her down because I wanted her to take me upstairs and show me where the baby was located. I told my company to start stretching a hose line upstairs and went up with the woman. When we got to the third floor, I could see the fire.

"Smoke was pushing under the front door from pressure built up inside the apartment. I tried to open the door, but it was locked. Using my shoulder, I tried to force the door open without success. I asked my crew to bring up an entry tool."

Captain Pritchard knew he needed to ventilate the room as soon as a hose line was in place. This would have to be done from the outside and was the job of the outside vent man, or OVM. He contacted the OVM on the radio and told him to try and open a vent on one of the exterior windows on a fire escape. By establishing a vent to the outside, the fire could be controlled and the interior heat reduced. The mother told him again that her child was trapped in the apartment. But the intense heat of the fire had already blown the windows out.

"Time was so important, and I knew we didn't have any to spare. I thought if I hit the door harder, I might be able to force it open. Just as I was about to hit the door again, I noticed that the mother had actually left the keys in the door.

"When I opened the door, the hallway was immediately filled with thick, black smoke. The hallway banked all the way to the floor almost immediately. The mother had described the interior layout of the apartment to me and where Shadae's crib was located. I told her to stay in the hallway."

Because what had been originally a living room was converted into a bedroom, there were two bedrooms in the apartment. When Pritchard went inside, he was in a small entryway and had to turn to his right and then move around a short wall and back to the left to gain access to the converted living room where the baby was.

"I dropped to the floor and started crawling. I got word that the outside vent man couldn't make it in by the fire escape because the fire was already venting out of those windows. It was either going to be me or she was gone. I couldn't wait for a line to be advanced up the stairs. It wasn't that the crew wasn't hurrying, it was just that there was no more time.

"I had taken my gloves off to open the door, and I didn't put them back on in my haste to get into the room. I could hear the cries of the baby. She was calling to me.

"I asked God to give me the strength to push ahead. 'Oh God, just another foot.' The whole room was filled with flames. Every inch hurt so much. The flames were all around me by then. Still she was crying, calling to me. When I got halfway through the room, which was only fifteen feet deep, I came to the limit of what I could do. Then she cried again. It was the little voice of a baby in the face of death calling out. 'Oh God, help me please,' I asked again.

"Then I came to the playpen. I could see the little girl now. Just behind her, the fire was already down to the baseboard and the flames were hovering just inches above the top rail."

By now, the bed in the room was on fire. The dresser was burning, and the walls were in flames. The venting path for the flames was out the windows just over Shadae's sleeping place, her playpen. To Captain Pritchard, the baby wasn't crying out in pain—she was calling him to save her.

"I couldn't reach over and get her because it meant standing up in a massive blowtorch. I knew that if I didn't make it, she wouldn't either. By then I couldn't even crawl; I was lying prone on the floor. I raised myself up to reach over, and my hand burned immediately."

Pritchard's safety equipment was starting to show the effects of the tremendous heat. His turnout coat was becoming discolored. The material around his SCBA facepiece was now melting and his helmet blistering as well.

"I was only inches from her, and yet it seemed like miles. Then I noticed she wasn't making any more sounds. That was when I knew I had to make a drastic move. I reached up and grabbed the top of the playpen and started to drag it. When I did, the plastic melted around my hand. It was so hot, the molten plastic was dripping down around me. I was being burned badly, but there was nothing else I could do.

"I had fought my way in there, and now it was going to be another battle to get out, but I had something to show for it. I had Shadae Brophete, and we were heading for the doorway. I began yelling, 'Help me! Help me! I have the baby. I have the baby.'

"I wanted my crew to hear me and answer back, which would give me something to home in on. The next thing I knew, they grabbed me and pulled me into the hallway."

Firefighter Michael King took Shadae from the playpen and ran with her down the hallway to the stairs. Her clothes were burned, and she was unconscious when he pulled her out. He gave her to the paramedics.

Captain Pritchard had suffered third-degree burns to his hands and was in tremendous pain, but there was still fire to fight. The firefighters of Engine 255 entered the building, pulling an inch-and-three-quarter hose up four flights of stairs; they were ready to attack the fire. Refus-

ing medical treatment, their captain took up a place on the hose, grab-
bing it with his burned hands, and in they went. He was concerned that
there could be other children in the apartment.

"Before 255 got up to us, Firefighter George Shea went to the right,
passing the room filled with fire, and headed back into the rear of the
apartment. There wasn't any fire back there, but there was the same
heavy, black smoke and he found a second child—six-year-old Actura
Powell.

"After we knocked the fire down, I told my crew that I had to go to
the hospital. The pain was becoming unbearable by then. When I got
to the hospital burn unit, they were working on Shadae. She had burns
to more than 50 percent of her body. One whole side of her body from
head to toe was burned. She was only ten months old, and she spent the
next eight months in the hospital."

Captain Pritchard had burns on his face, wrists, and hands of vary-
ing degrees, with the most severe, third-degree burns, to his hands.
He spent the next seven days in the burn unit and did not return to
work for three months. While he was in the unit, Shadae's mother and
grandmother came by to see him and thanked him for saving their little girl.

Battalion Chief Isaiah Johnson wrote a Report of Meritorious Act
(the first stage in the process of bestowing a medal for heroism on an
FDNY member) about Captain Pritchard and said, "There is no doubt
that this child would not have survived were it not for the heroic effort
of Captain Pritchard. He placed himself in extreme danger in effecting
this rescue." Anyone who knew the captain was not at all surprised by
his actions. It was not his first brush with death to result in an award for
valor. It was actually his ninth.

The FDNY gives several medals for heroic acts each year, the highest of which is the Gordon Bennett Medal. For a firefighter to receive
this medal in the course of a career would be remarkable. Captain
Pritchard has two.

Each medal awarded by the FDNY falls into one of three classes of
meritorious acts, the highest being Class One. To qualify, a firefighter

must have been exposed to "extreme personal risk." This is the kind of risk that means death to the rescuer is not just possible, but likely. It had been nine years since a Class One medal had been awarded. For the rescue of the baby, the medal committee recognized Captain John Pritchard not only with his second Gordon Bennett Medal, but they made it a Class One as well.

It is a rare member of the FDNY to have any medal categorized as a Class One. Captain Pritchard is the only member of the department to have received three at this level. Each one bought him time in the burn center.

The other two classes of medals are awarded for "great personal risk" and "unusual personal risk." Captain Pritchard has a total of five of these.

Captain Pritchard was also given a top Medal for Valor from *Firehouse* magazine as part of their Heroism and Community Service program.

When asked about all the burns he received over the years, he said, "You have to prepare yourself as a firefighter and say to yourself that this is normal. You say this is what separates the people who are running out from the firefighters who are running in. You understand that the consequences of not going in outweigh the ones if you do go in.

"I'm a battalion chief now, and as you go up the ranks, you take on a different perspective. Now my job is to protect my firefighters and make sure they're safe. You understand risk management, we know we have to do it, but let's not do it for nothing. Make sure the reward is going to be worth the risk. But it must be remembered there is no rescue without the support of an entire crew. In my case it was the dedicated firefighters of Engine 255 who were there for me."

I asked if it had been worth it for him, and without hesitation he said, "It always has been."

The rewards left in the wake of John Pritchard's valorous acts are easy to measure. So many times he was willing to sacrifice every tomorrow he had to give somebody one more of his or her own. When Shadae's mother looks into the eyes of her little girl, she understands.

10

"I WAS ON FIRE"

March 15, 2000

St. Louis, Missouri

Lee Little and Rick Snow

Engine 34's Captain Rick Snow and his crew were only about four blocks away from the fire that had broken out at 7710 Alabama Street. The caller said two people might be trapped inside. The captain was not just any firefighter—he was one of the most decorated on the St. Louis Fire Department.

Lee Little had recently been assigned to Engine 23 and was working only his fourth day there. Normally, that station was considered quiet, in fact one of the quietest in the city. Engine 23 was also dispatched to the fire. They were farther away and did not arrive as quickly as Snow's company.

When Snow's company pulled up, flames were showing from the windows on what appeared to be the front of the house. It was deceptive because the front of the residence actually faced away from the

**Lee Little,
St. Louis Fire Department.**

**Rick Snow,
St. Louis Fire Department.**

street. As Captain Snow got off his truck, he told the firefighters to get a line ready.

"I ran around to what I thought was the back of the house to assess the situation," remembers Snow. "When I got around to the rear, I discovered it was actually the front. There was a woman screaming that her kids were in the second-floor apartment. Her screams were horrible."

The building was actually an old schoolhouse, which was why there was no street-side access. When it was converted to a dwelling, it was designed to have two apartments on the first floor and two on the second. The only access to the second floor was via an outside set of wooden stairs.

"The stairs appeared to be in very bad repair, but it was up them or nothing. At the top of the stairs was an open door leading to where her children were. She screamed again, 'They're in there!' I can't describe the way she screamed. It was a cry of total desperation.

"But there was a big problem too. Flames were pouring out through the door. It looked really bad. Again she cried out. It was a plea to me to save her babies. I knew if I went in that door, I might not come out. But what could I do? It wasn't about me at that point, it was about them.

"As I went up the stairs, I put out a call to the other units and let them know what we had. When I got to the top, I knelt down to escape the heat and flames. I had on my SCBA, but I hadn't put on my facepiece yet. As I got ready to go in, I took off my helmet and pulled up my Nomex hood. Then I positioned my facepiece and checked everything again to make sure I didn't have any exposed skin.

"I got down on my stomach and crawled in. I felt like I was in the middle of hell, it was so hot in there. The heat was coming through my helmet, my boots—everywhere. Even though I had all my safety gear on, I was still getting burned from the heat coming up through the floor.

"I knew if I was going to make it I had to rush. The only way the kids were going to have a chance was for me to do it right. I was crawling as fast as I could. I looked into a room on my left and could see it was a bedroom."

The smoke was not too thick because it was being consumed by the flames. The house and its contents were burning up in an efficient and very hot fire.

Downstairs, Engine 23 had just arrived. They had all their safety gear on and were ready when they stepped off the truck. Lee Little listened to the chatter on the radio as they were en route.

"Even though I was new to the company, the other firefighters knew the address and we discussed the place while we were on our way to the call. I knew it was going to be bad when we got there. I could hear Captain Snow on the radio. I knew him from working the sixth district with him. We had worked several fires together in there, and I recognized his voice over the radio. He never got excited; he was always very calm, but not then. He was very hyper, and I knew he was in a bad situation. I was glad he was there, because he would know what to do."

Snow's company would be the first to put water on the fire. In addition, two men would normally perform search and rescue while the captain led them. But they were short a man and would have to approach the fire differently.

"When we got to the house, we went around to the back and intended on putting up ladders to the second floor, but with the stairs we didn't need to, and we prepared to go up the stairs and ventilate the second floor. Captain Snow was inside on the second floor."

Inside, Snow continued checking the bedroom. He looked under the bed, thinking a child might go there in search of refuge from the flames and heat, but he found no one. He raised himself up to check the top of the bed.

"When I raised up, I got hit with a tremendous blast of heat. The plastic part of my mask started waving like water. It was melting. I could see flames coming around my head. Then I realized my hood was on fire too. I was in real trouble. I dropped down and tried to crawl out of the room, but I got lost for about ten or fifteen seconds.

"I figured out where I was, and I had to get out. I was on fire and it hurt. I started yelling to my crew that I was on fire."

Little came up the stairs and heard a commotion at the top. Looking up, he was shocked at what he saw.

"I could see Captain Snow coming out. I thought, Oh my God, what's going on here? This was Rick Snow, the most decorated firefighter on the department, and he was in flames. The mother was down at the bottom of the stairs, screaming that her children were trapped inside. As Captain Snow ran past me, the woman's voice rang in my ears.

"If the fire got him, how could we go in? There was no time to think about what to do. As Snow passed us he told us he saw people in the right bedroom. I grabbed his coat and tried to get it off of him. He fell into the arms of other firefighters who took the burning gear off him. I saw them take him to the medic unit."

Other firefighters stripped him of his burning gear. Snow was careful to stay away from the paramedics and the chief. "If they had seen me I would have been finished for the day. My crew wet down my coat just enough to get rid of the fire." It was imperative that all the fire was extinguished before he put it back on.

On the second floor, Little entered the apartment. He remembered what Snow had said: "I think I saw them to the right." Sam Brownfield and Dave Smith from Engine 34 advanced a line into the apartment and began to attack the fire. Harvey Jackson, the engineer and driver, stayed with the engine and made sure the water supply remained adequate. The two firefighters went to the right as they entered the apartment. Lee Little went to the left.

"I don't know why I went the way I did. There were children in that place, and we had to find them because they were going to die if we didn't. I had a pike pole with me, and I began breaking windows to vent the bedroom to get some of the smoke and heat out. The smoke was much heavier in that room and was banked down to within two feet of the floor, and it was hot."

Out in the driveway, Captain Snow inspected his coat and put it on. Securing his helmet and Nomex hood, he climbed the stairs and went back into the fire.

"I knew my crew was up there and I was in charge of them," Snow remembers. "One of them was a kid. How could I make sure they were safe if I was talking to the paramedics? My tank was out of air so I dropped it on the ground. When I got to the top of the stairs I tucked my face into my coat to protect myself and get some good air to breathe and went in. The firefighter on the nozzle was a rookie, and this was his first big fire. I was worried that something might happen to him."

Lee Little saw Captain Snow come back into the apartment, and he wasn't totally surprised. Snow was a firefighter's captain; he led by example—that was the kind of firefighter he was. Little knew that Snow was the epitome of the firefighter he wanted to be. Little remembers, "When I saw Rick back in there, I was somewhat relieved because with his knowledge, he would keep us from getting into too much trouble."

Little and five or six firefighters searched the apartment. Firefighter Smith and Captain Snow fought back the flames. Outside, the flames had spread to the building next door and an all-clear was sounded, which meant that the officer in command of the fire ground believed the situation had become untenable for the firefighters. The fire ground commander decided to evacuate the firefighters, and at that time, they were all ordered out of or away from the structure.

"By this time, my burns were really starting to hurt," Snow remembers. "My coat was badly damaged, I wasn't getting the protection I needed, and the heat was getting to me. We waited outside for a few minutes while more water was put on the fire, and it was determined that we could go back in. I thought I had seen a baby in one of the rooms to the right, but it was burning so hot in there we hadn't been able to get in there yet."

Little went back in and searched again. It was later determined that the temperature in that the room was between 1,000 to 1,500 degrees. He kept searching.

"The venting and water had lowered the temperature," Little remembers. "They were definitely knocking down the fire at that point. I was on my hands and knees crawling. I went into the same bedroom Snow had first searched. I checked under the bed and on top of it. I looked in every corner and found a closet and checked it out. Then, I searched behind it. There was no one in that room, so I left and went out in the hall.

"I went into the kitchen next and began to do a search. Then an all-clear horn was sounded, and I had to leave the building. We were losing the battle again. Even though where I was searching wasn't bad, other parts of the house were very involved."

By now, several companies had responded. At this point, no one had been found, and the apartment was beginning to flame again. The all-clear was sounded for fear that the house might collapse, taking several firefighters with it. Several companies continued to do battle from the outside in an effort to gain the upper hand again. It worked, and in a few minutes the fire that was showing through the roof had subsided.

"As soon as we got permission, we went back in. They let us go back in two and three at a time. It was worse than when we left, but Captain Snow and Smith began attacking the fire again," Little remembers. "I went back into the bedroom and searched again. As a firefighter, you don't go back and search the same place over and over, and we had thoroughly searched this room. I knew this, but I just felt pulled back there, and I don't know why. I felt I had to search one more time. Under the bed, on top of the bed, and in the closet—nothing. This time, another firefighter and I flipped the mattress up against the wall. There was nothing under it. We took it out and put it in the hallway.

"I went around all the corners of the room and then into the closet. Again, I went through the toy box and found nothing. Once again I headed out to the hallway. We still hadn't found the missing baby.

"There was a lot of noise in there. Everybody had their radios on, and that, coupled with the sound of the fire and the spraying water, made it hard to hear. As I got to the doorway, I heard something. It sounded like a cat, but not in that room; the heat had been too intense.

"I turned off my radio and stayed there on the floor, listening. Then I heard it a second time. Then it was quiet again. It was hard to tell where the sound was coming from, so I went back to the closet again.

"I went through all the contents on the floor—nothing. The smoke had gotten thicker again, and I couldn't see a thing. I went into the toy box again. I already had my hands to the bottom of this box three times before. I started digging in the box, taking things out. I moved this big teddy bear and I thought it was a person at first. I was really excited, thinking I had found the child. Then I realized it was only a stuffed animal, so I grabbed it and threw it out.

"As I pulled my hand up to toss the bear, I made contact with something else. I let go of the bear and put my hands in. There was the baby and he was still alive. It was like he was saying, 'I'm barely alive, but I need out.'

"I picked him up and then I heard a rush of sound as the ceiling collapsed. Plaster and burning wood rained down on us. When it came down, I pulled the baby close to my stomach. I couldn't go anywhere until it finished collapsing."

When the cascade of fire and debris finished falling on Little and the child, he stood up and ran for the door. From the outside, everyone saw Little, still covered with burning debris, carrying a little child. All of the searching had paid off for Little. The three-year-old boy was alive. He turned him over to the paramedics and headed back into the fire.

They all stayed and fought the fire until it was knocked down. While Little was not burned, Captain Snow was not as fortunate. He had burns on much of his face and upper body but his turnout gear had kept them to a minimum. The most serious were second-degree burns on his ears. He left the scene only after being ordered to do so by the fire chief. He was transported to the hospital by ambulance along with the child rescued by Little.

For Captain Snow and the other firefighters, the fire at Alabama Street holds bitter memories. Two children were in fact trapped in that apartment. The other child was in the room that Snow couldn't get into because of the flames. Even though the room was consumed by fire and Captain Snow was too, the child was lost, and in his mind, he was to blame. It didn't matter that it was totally engulfed with fire. The unspeakably horrible sight of the little baby who perished and the belief that somehow he could have done more are etched in his memory. Even today, he speaks through his tears when he talks about the fire that day.

Both Rick Snow and Lee Little were awarded the Medal of Valor from the St. Louis Fire Department. They were also awarded Medals for Valor by *Firehouse* magazine as part of their Heroism and Community Service program. This was not the first time the captain had been so decorated. He previously saved two firefighters who were trapped in a burning building. Another award for heroism came after he snatched a man from certain death at a house fire. He is quick to point out that he wasn't alone and without his crew, he couldn't have done anything.

Though Captain Snow is hard on himself, he does not extend this criticism to Lee Little. "I don't think I am a hero. I just had good people with me to protect me if something happened. Little is the hero. He did so much more than I was able to do."

When I asked Captain Snow to do an interview for this book, he was very hesitant, saying he didn't think he belonged with the other "real" heroes in the book.

He was wrong. He does.

11

IT'S JUST BUSINESS

May 30, 1990

Boston, Massachusetts

Edward T. Loder

"Boston Fire Press Relations."

"Hi. This is Eddie Loder."

"Oh, sorry Eddie, we don't have any medals today for you. Talk to you later." Click. Loder just laughs and calls them back to conduct business. This isn't the first time Loder has called Boston Fire Department Press Relations and has gotten his chops busted. It is all lighthearted, but what else could be expected when Edward T. Loder, the most decorated firefighter in the history of the Boston Fire Department, happens to call?

Loder works Rescue 1 and has been decorated six times for valor, including five Roll of Merits and a Walter Scott Medal of Valor. In addition, Loder was awarded two Medals of Valor from the commonwealth of Massachusetts. He couldn't be more dedicated when he is called to business. Business for Loder—his friends call him "Eddie"—is rescuing people when it seems impossible. The most extreme rescue Loder and

Edward T. Loder, Boston Fire Department.

his crew participated in involved a woman who was crushed beneath a dumpster truck after a collision. The truck had cut the woman in half, but the weight of the truck was preventing her from bleeding to death. The firefighters knew that once the truck was lifted the woman would die. They crawled under the vehicle, as it was lifted off of her, to comfort her in the last moments of her life. That rescue earned them a unit citation.

The Ritz-Carlton Hotel at 15 Arlington Street in Boston is renowned for its five-star accommodations and outstanding service; certainly the last thing the staff and its guests would expect is a woman threatening to plunge to her death from her room, sixteen stories above the posh lobby.

When Rescue 1 arrived, Loder, using a pair of binoculars, was able to make out the shape of the woman in the dimly lit conditions. Inside, police officers and hotel staff had been attempting, without success, to coax her from her very precarious perch on the ledge of her room's window.

Lieutenant John Joyce was in charge of Rescue 1 that night, and he directed his men to set up an air jump bag in the street. This is a large, inflatable, square bag developed by stunt people in the movie industry. The idea was to position it to catch her if she jumped.

District Fire Chief Stephen Dunbar was also at the scene and sent the lieutenant to the sixteenth floor to check things out and devise a plan. When he got up there, he learned that the woman was standing in the corner of her hotel room, which would allow her to see the firefighters coming in the door from the hallway. She was in a corner room, which meant any attempt to come in from the side and in one of her windows would give her ample time to jump out the other window. The only option was to descend from the roof and tackle her to safety.

Rescue 1 members James Hardy, Robert Breen, Paul Carey, and Edward Loder, along with Ladder 17 crew members Lieutenant Michael Walsh and Firefighters Thomas Bell, Reynolds Sheperd, and Paul Minton, were ordered to the roof to see if such a plan would be feasible.

"We had started up to the sixteenth floor when they told us to go back and bring rope with us," Loder remembers. "Our original plan of attack was to talk with her. But when the lieutenant and district chief got up there, they found the Boston Police Department, which had a team trained to negotiate with suicidal people—but it was having little success. A rope rescue became our only feasible alternative. I went up to the roof and thought I would play my part while somebody did the rescue. They had the bag in place, but it was only rated to handle a person falling from six to seven stories."

A parapet was at the edge of the roof of the Ritz-Carlton. In addition to extending upward, it also went out from the edge of the building about a foot, protecting the firefighters from being detected by the distraught woman.

"We looked over the edge and you couldn't see anything. We were just above her room. She was about ten feet below us, and she hadn't a clue. I was carrying the rope bag when we went up to the roof. Everyone was talking about how we were going to do this. The consensus was to go down from the top and directly into the window. Then the discussion turned to who was going to go over the side. All of a sudden everyone looked at me. I looked around at all of them and said, 'Well, I'm holding the rope. So, I guess it's me. Plus I'm the lightest guy here anyway.' Everybody just broke up laughing and several of them said, 'Well, OK.'

"The next order of business was to find a place to anchor the rope. There was a one-story room on the rooftop that held mechanical gear for the elevators. It had a couple of windows. We went into the room and decided the corner of the building was the best anchor point. We put the rope through one of the windows and out the door to make a loop. Since I was the one going over, I made sure the anchor point was good. It wasn't likely that I would drag the building over the side.

"At that time, we had what was called a 'bumblebee suit' to wear for this kind of rescue. It was actually a jacket with D rings attached to the outside of it, which the ropes were anchored on to. The plan was to divert her attention away from the window, and then I would go over the edge. I knew we had no time to mess around when I went down. It had to be quick and seamless. If I got down in front of the window and couldn't get in, I'd have to struggle with her, which didn't interest me at all."

While the firefighters on the roof were making preparations for their part, the negotiators were still trying to bring the situation to a close without needing to endanger a firefighter. They discovered that the woman had been a patient at a psychiatric hospital, and the police officers were able to get her doctor on the telephone.

The psychiatrist's words were not encouraging. He told them if they planned to do anything, it better be done quickly because she definitely would go out the window. Time had always been of the essence, but now the situation appeared even more dire.

"We were still strategizing up on the roof when we heard that it had to be done right away because she could jump at any second. We knew the approximate distance down to the window and laid out the same length of rope on the roof. That was going to be how much the guys on the line would feed out."

In a call such as this, the nearest ladder company is sent to back up the rescue company, and that night it was Ladder 17. Lieutenant Walsh was in charge and on the roof as Loder put on the "bumblebee." Loder and Walsh were good friends who went back many years. Just as Loder was finishing his preparation to go over the side, the lieutenant walked over to him.

"Eddie, are you sure you want to do this?"

Loder looked up from the rope he was checking and responded with a smile on his face. "No, I don't want to do this at all."

"Listen, you want me to go downstairs and get a bottle from the bar and maybe you can have a couple of drinks before you go?" Walsh joked. "Maybe one of those high-class hookers walking down there? I could get one for you too. You know, in case the rope snaps, you could go out with all the glory."

Loder paused a moment as if to consider the proposal. "Naw, let's just get it done."

Then the radio came alive again with word from the woman's doctor that she was becoming very agitated. She was stating she had waited long enough and was going to jump. Loder knew he had to go.

"I was going to do it all in one motion. I was going to look over the side and while the police diverted her attention away from the window, I would come flying in through it. I got in place at the edge of the parapet that would act as my launching pad and watched. I also told my crew to tell the police what I was going to do. They had to be ready as I went so they could move in and grab her. Then Lieutenant Joyce came over to talk to me."

Joyce said, "Oh, there's one more thing I forgot to tell you. She's got a razor in her hand."

"I said, 'What?' This kept getting worse. Then I told him that I wasn't going to treat her with kid gloves. All I could picture was her, razor in hand, taking a big swipe at my rope. Then I pictured my plunge to the street. I was going to come in feetfirst and hopefully I would kick her back into the room.

"I was looking down at her and then she looked away and I told them to tell everyone I was coming down. I said, 'All right, let's go for it.' Over I went. The rope was slack as I fell from the roof. I kind of went out in an arc and when the rope tightened it pulled me back toward the window. It went just as we had planned.

"She must have seen some movement out of the corner of her eye just as I was about to crash through the window because she let out a scream. My boots made contact with her side and she flew into the arms of the police who were running toward her.

"She never saw it coming and she was furious. When I plowed into her, the razor in her hand went flying. One second she was sitting there telling us to stay away or she would jump, and in the next, the police were swarming over her.

"It worked flawlessly. Almost. The forward motion I had was totally absorbed when I hit her. She flew away from the window and I went back the other way. As I watched them dive on her, I was dangling sixteen stories above the street. There was nothing I could do.

"I yelled in to them, 'Hey, don't forget about me.' One of the officers came over and pulled me inside.

"As they stood her up, she looked back at me and let me know what a good job I had done. She called me a 'fucking asshole' as they led her away.

"I went downstairs and I was shaking a little bit. All the police officers came over and congratulated me. Even the mayor was there talking to the news media. I heard him tell them, 'Yeah, I know that guy. He's a hell of a firefighter, that Loder.' Maybe he was exaggerating a little, but it was nice for him to say anyway.

"That was a nice rescue," Loder remembers. "It worked just the way it was supposed to. Everybody played a part. I was just one person. It couldn't have happened without everyone there. The news stories were written about me, but the rescue was everybody's."

For his efforts, Edward Loder received the Walter Scott Medal of Valor, and the Medal of Valor from the commonwealth of Massachusetts. He also received a Medal for Valor from *Firehouse* magazine as part of the Heroism and Community Service program.

The Ritz-Carlton turned out to be a practice session for another high rescue. On April 16, 1993, another person was ready to terminate his life. This time it was on the roof of Boston City Hospital.

It was a bit after eleven in the morning, and a man had positioned himself on the roof of the seven-story Dowling Building at Boston City Hospital. Ladder 15 responded, as did Rescue 1. The idea was to put the aerial ladder up to the roof where the man was perched.

When the call came out, Rescue 1 was at fire headquarters picking up some gear, and Loder was driving the rescue unit that day. "They told us to get over to Boston Hospital. We were only a few blocks from the call so we got there very quickly. Ladder 17 also got sent along with 15. We had a lot of people there. In addition, the Boston Police were there and inside the hospital, the hospital staff was talking to the man on the roof.

"When the ladder companies pulled up, the guy got really agitated and began throwing gravel down from the roof on the fire trucks below.

Whenever you have an incident like this, a district chief is sent to the scene. Chief John Kinney got there, and he took a look at the situation and asked us, 'What can you do for this guy?'

"I said to him, 'Well, he's up on the roof. It's a pretty big roof. If we get an observation post, we can find out what he is up to or what side he is on and we could kind of look the situation over.' I also told him, 'If you put the aerial up between this building and the other one, maybe that will drive him to the other one.' On the opposite side was another building, but there was a twenty- to thirty-foot gap between them."

Ladder 17 had also been dispatched and was in place; they raised their aerial ladder up to the roof. They intended to send a firefighter up there to talk to the man. Before a firefighter could scale the seven stories, the distraught man threatened to jump if they did not lower the ladder immediately.

Loder thought it would be a good idea if they took 15's ladder and put it up on the opposite side of the building. "I figured he might run away from 17's ladder and over to 15's. I told them I would go up to the tip of the ladder and try to talk to this guy. So I went up and sure enough, he came over.

"He was pretty upset when he saw me and said he was going to jump. He was in his twenties, and I didn't know it at the time, but he was a patient in the hospital. I said to him, 'Look, why don't we just sit down and have a cup of coffee and talk about this? We'll talk about it, have a cigarette, and find out what drove you to something like this. What's going wrong for you? You got a problem with your wife or girlfriend or something like that?'

"I'm only about seven or eight feet away from where he was standing. This went on for about an hour. I just kept talking to him. He was looking at me, but not paying much attention.

"He never actually told me what his problem was. I was sort of holding up both sides of the conversation. Then I said to him, 'Listen, I'm getting tired of sitting up here, trying to baby-sit you. It's lunchtime, I'm hungry, and I want to eat. What about it, we'll go and have lunch. You and I. . . .' He cut me off and said, 'I don't want no lunch. I'm going to kill myself!'

"I looked him in the eye and said, 'Listen, if you were going to do that, you would have done it two hours ago. I don't think you're serious about it.' Mistake! I was trying to get him to look at what he was doing to try and defuse the situation. That wasn't exactly what I did. He climbed over the side and started to walk along a pipe affixed to the building, holding onto the parapet. I told him, 'You're going to lose your footing and fall. Why don't you turn around and go back up where you were?'

"By now I was very close to him, and I said that I could turn him around and help him back up. With that he spun around, and he let go of the edge of the building with one hand. He pulled his other arm out of his jacket. Then he reached and grabbed the pipe again. As he did that, he let go with his other hand. Then he pulled off his jacket and threw it down to the street below.

"And then he jumped. I just reached out and grabbed him. When I latched onto him, I ended up with his shirt in my hand and he was hanging about seventy feet in the air. I wasn't prepared for him to do what he did, and I came very close to going off my ladder with him. At the last second, I was able to hook my leg around a rung of the ladder."

When Loder grabbed the man, the strain of the additional weight pulled the ladder down suddenly. The force caused the ladder truck to tilt with one side coming off the ground. It was a very anxious moment until the truck settled back down.

"Larry Holt, a firefighter who was down at the base of the ladder, ran up with a life belt and hooked it to me and then to the ladder. I should have put one on myself before, but I really was expecting just to talk to him.

"Now I was hanging onto the ladder with one hand and I had him hanging below me with the other. I have no idea how I was able to keep a hold on him. I had always heard of superhuman strength in times of crisis and I guess this was an example of it.

"There was a young firefighter on the turntable control for the ladder. He hit the wrong control and instead of rotating me away from the building, he went the wrong way. My arm was between the ladder and the building and what must have been hundreds of pounds of force crushed my arm. Fortunately, it was the arm I was holding onto the ladder with and not the other. If it had been the arm I was grasping the man with, he would have fallen to his death. As it was, he was swinging back and forth as the ladder moved.

"The guy isn't saying a word. He was just dangling there, as quiet as could be. If it were me, I would have been screaming at the top of my lungs. Then the ladder started to lower. There wasn't any way I could do anything but hold on. It would have been impossible to pull him up onto the ladder. I was afraid to do anything with him. I was just concentrating on keeping my grip."

Slowly the ladder was lowered toward the ground. Loder didn't move and neither did the mentally disturbed man. When they got down to about thirty feet, Loder started to have trouble.

"My hand was starting to cramp up. It hurt, but at the same time it was sort of numb. I was able to last until we got below ten feet. I finally couldn't hold on anymore and he slipped from my grip, falling about seven to eight feet. He didn't get a scratch. I wished I could have said the same for myself."

Incredibly, Loder's crushed arm was not broken, although the open flesh wounds were quite bloody. Time for another trip to the hospital for Edward Loder, but since they were already there, it didn't take long.

For his actions, Edward T. Loder was awarded the Roll of Merit medal for valor. He has received this particular award five times.

12

"MY SERGEANT IS NOT WITH ME"

October 24, 1997

Washington, District of Columbia

John Carter and Kenneth Crosswhite

It was a mild fall in the District, and late October finally did bring in the chilly temperatures. And, as is usually the case, the first cold weather brought a spate of heating-related problems. When a call came in to Engine 22 at 6:20 that morning, Washington, D.C., Fire Lieutenant Kenneth Crosswhite didn't think too much about it.

"We were the off-going shift that morning, and I was waiting for my relief. When the call came in, I figured it was the first cold day of the month, and there are a lot of oil burners in the neighborhood. I thought it was probably a blast of smoke coming from a burner that had just been fired up. Since the other shift had not come in yet, we headed out to the call.

Kenneth Crosswhite,
Washington, D.C., Fire Department.

John Carter,
Washington, D.C., Fire Department.

"Before we got to the building, word came over the radio indicating that we had a working fire. When we pulled up, we saw it was a two-story building. On the first floor was a grocery store with an apartment above. The fire was in the grocery store."

Truck 11 was also dispatched to the call. The store owner met the firefighters when they arrived. He had already raised the roll-up security doors, giving them access to the building. From the outside, it appeared that the fire was on the first floor in the back of the building.

"We went into the store and down the first right-side aisle, all the way to the back. We couldn't find any fire. Firefighter Carl Parker was with me, and I told him to wait there. He had a charged line with him. I asked him if he had a flashlight and he said he didn't. 'I'm going to crawl ahead about forty feet or so,' I said to him. 'I'll put my flashlight down on the floor when I turn onto another aisle.' I crawled down that aisle and made a turn. I put my light down as a marker. As soon as I made my turn, I saw the fire. I called back to him to come toward me and that I had found the fire. I told him to open his nozzle up and play it across the ceiling. I was concerned about the temperature in the room and the possibility of a flashover.

"Steve Mills, a firefighter from Truck 11, made his way into the building and met up with us. I told him to stay with us and we would operate as a company. We were down a firefighter that day, and he would bring us up to the number we needed.

"At one point, I noticed a beautiful blue flame come across the ceiling. I notified the battalion chief that we had the possibility of a gas fire and advised him that we needed to have the gas main shut off. Carl Parker kept the stream on the ceiling, which prevented the fire from getting behind us, but at the same time didn't put it out."

If the blue flame on the ceiling was a gas fire and it was extinguished, there would have been a great likelihood of an explosion. Up to this point, Lieutenant Crosswhite and the other firefighters had tolerable conditions inside the market. He ordered the building to be opened up to lower the interior temperature and vent the smoke.

"Engine 24 was the 'second due' company, which meant they were responsible for entry into the basement. I hadn't heard a status report from them. Then, in a matter of a minute, everything changed. Canned goods started exploding. Floor tiles were popping off of the floor. I knew right then we had a fire beneath us and it was time to immediately back out of the building.

"I asked the company what the status of the basement was. They radioed back they were unable to gain access. I ordered everyone out of the building at once. I knew we had to get out and do it quickly.

"The temperature was rising fast. Soup cans flew around like missiles as they exploded. At that time, I believed only three of us were in the store. I told Parker to hold onto the shut-off valve while I held the tip of the line and we would back out with me being the last one on the line. As we made our way out down the aisle, cans were exploding all over.

"Then I found out that Steve Mills had not come out ahead of us. He was tangled in the hose. I told Parker to grab the nozzle and that I was going to go back around and check on Mills. When I got to him I said, 'What's up? What's wrong?' He said, 'I've been hit.' It didn't register with me, and I asked him what he meant, and he told me a flying can had gotten him in the head."

After being struck in the head with a can, Mills had fallen in the hose that was being pulled out by Crosswhite and Parker. It was twisted around his legs. With the temperature rapidly rising, Crosswhite worked quickly to free the firefighter.

"When I finally got him free of the hose, I asked him if he could crawl out. He said he could, so I told him the front door was only about fifteen or twenty feet from where he was, then I went back to Carl to help him get the hose out of there.

"The heat was starting to be a real problem by now. When I got back to Parker, he had fallen partially through the floor. The fire had eaten through. What had seemed to go from bad to worse was now beyond that.

"He was stuck in the hole with flames coming up around him. I stepped into the flames and grabbed onto him. I pulled while he struggled to free himself, and he was out. It was fortunate that I came back when I did. I was really in the right place and time to help him.

"During this time period, the fire department was in a serious budget crisis. When things were broken, they weren't replaced. We didn't have any spare hoses. If we lost a hose in a fire, that was it. The hose was gone and there wouldn't be any replacements. It was the same way for our communication system. When a radio broke, getting it fixed was very difficult and if it couldn't be repaired, then we simply had one less. Firefighters in Washington, D.C., bought things for the firehouse out of their own money during that time.

"But the hose was no longer important. I knew the room was going to be filled with flames any second. I made a decision to abandon the hose and exit directly. We quickly made our way through the smoke-filled aisles and out the front door. The visibility was near zero as we went through the front door.

"As soon as we got out to the sidewalk, I knew I had all of my people. But what really threw me off was the number of firefighters lying in complete exhaustion on the sidewalk. They had also been inside the store and were absolutely wiped out by the heat. We had been in different parts of the store and I never saw any of them inside.

"In less than a minute after we got outside, the whole first floor of the building rolled over."

A rollover occurs when the unburned particles in the smoke reach a temperature point that supports combustion. It is similar to a flashover, only the contents of the room do not burn. The fire in a rollover lasts as long as it takes for the airborne particles to burn, and then the thick, black smoke comes back. In a flashover, the room and its contents keep burning. Either occurrence will kill the occupant of the room.

There was not a shred of doubt that Lieutenant Crosswhite had reacted correctly to the situation. The building heat and deteriorating conditions spelled disaster for him and the two firefighters with him. His decision to abandon the building and hose more than likely saved all of their lives. When the lieutenant was asked what would have happened if they decided to retrieve the hose, he didn't hesitate in responding, "We don't make it."

"There was a new battalion chief at the scene and I walked over to him, intending to give him a status report. As I got close to him, a firefighter from Engine 14 came up and said, 'My sergeant is not with me.'

"I asked him what he was talking about. He told me that he had gotten separated from Sergeant John Carter. Engine 14 was the third truck to the scene. My men and I were inside by the time they got there. Carter and another firefighter had been inside together, off to the left of the front door. This explained why we didn't see them, as we were to the right. Sergeant Carter decided to evacuate the building. When that happened, the firefighter came out with the hose and thought his sergeant had followed him.

"I told him to look around and make sure his sergeant wasn't sitting outside with everyone else. Then he told me he had looked everywhere and the sergeant was not there. He believed he was still inside.

"Looking at Battalion Chief Mansfield, I said, 'We're going back in.' There was an inch-and-a-half preconnect [a hose that is connected to the truck's water source and pump; it allows the firefighters to fight a fire immediately on arrival] lying on the sidewalk in front of the door. There was also a two-and-a-half already inside.

"My plan was to use the inch-and-a-half inside the doorway to protect us and to use the larger hose as a backup in case we had trouble and had to be rescued. Immediately, Lieutenants Larry Anderson and Henry Brooks along with Firefighter Lynn Parker said they were going in too.

"We didn't have an organized plan. We went in crawling on our stomachs. I went to the left, and they went to the right. I could see the fire coming up through the floor by the ice cream freezer. I crawled all the way down the side of the wall. I made it to the corner and tried to make the turn. I couldn't do it. The floor was mostly burned through. I came back to the front door and yelled for everyone to get out. I was fearful the floor would collapse.

"When one of your own is in there, you can't leave. You can't leave, because they wouldn't. We regrouped and made another entry, but it was no good. We couldn't get to the back of the store. I felt in my heart we were going to be able to rescue him, but we just had to take the right approach.

"The second time I thought we might be able to get past the corner, but the floor had collapsed into the basement. Any chance of proceeding that way was gone.

"After the second try, we listened for his PASS alarm or low-air alarm. We were trying to hear something that would give us an indication as to where he was located. We didn't hear anything.

"We went around to the side of the building and went in again. The majority of the floor was gone. Flames were coming out of the basement where the floor had collapsed. There wasn't any sign of Sergeant Carter.

"Then the radio brought the news and it wasn't good. We were to pull out of the building. The officers in charge had determined the structure was unsafe. We left and went around to the front. I thought we would get another assignment and then continue to look for a point of entry.

"There would be no new plan of attack, no last-second entry. The sergeant was gone. It didn't really sink in until they loaded us up and took us to the Metropolitan Police Department's homicide division." It is standard procedure to have them handle the questioning for any case involving a firefighter's death. There was no question of impropriety on the part of the firefighters.

The fire strategy changed from a search and rescue operation to that of a recovery. Later that morning, the body of the sergeant was recovered. The firefighter who had been with Carter recalled later that as he was pulling the hose out, he felt a tug for just a brief second and then it was gone. The hose pulled out normally, and when the last of it came out and the sergeant wasn't there, the firefighter assumed he had already come outside. That was when he checked around for Carter and discovered he was not among the firefighters who were sitting or lying on the sidewalk. Investigators would later conclude the tug happened when Carter fell through the floor into the basement. If the sergeant tried to call for help when he fell, it was useless. His radio didn't work.

Sergeant John Carter was posthumously awarded the Gold Medal of Valor and Lieutenant Kenneth Crosswhite received the Silver Medal of Valor. Kenneth also received the Mayor's Meritorious Service Award and was the Capital Exchange Firefighter of the Year.

In looking back on the whole incident, Crosswhite said, "If I had known that I was nominated for an award, I would have tried to persuade the officer who wrote the report not to do it. We lost a firefighter, and I didn't do anything that day any other firefighter wouldn't have done. I don't think I deserved the medal, but John Carter did."

It may be true that any other firefighter would have done the same thing, but there is little doubt that Lieutenant Kenneth Crosswhite did extraordinary things that morning. If not for his leadership and brave actions, the sadness of that day would likely have been much greater.

13

"I KNOW I'M GOING TO DROWN, BUT PLEASE DON'T LEAVE ME"

February 4, 1996

Santa Rosa, California

Donald Lopez and Dennis Rich

It had been raining for several days in Santa Rosa. Every once in a while, the clouds would break and the sun would come out, giving a ray of hope that the storm had passed. Not so. The sun quickly disappeared and it rained some more. On Sunday, February 4, 1996, more than four inches of rain fell, and the usually placid Matanzas Creek was a raging river.

At about 1:15 that afternoon, a call came into the Santa Rosa Fire Department. The caller said that two people were trapped in the creek. Firefighter Dennis Rich was working an overtime shift and driving Engine 4 that day. Also on the engine were Firefighter Greg McCollum and Captain Tim Hamlin.

Donald Lopez,
Santa Rosa, California, Fire Department.

Dennis Rich,
Santa Rosa, California, Fire Department.

"I was pretty familiar with that area, and I knew there was a creek behind the apartment complex off of Bethards Drive," Rich explains. "When I pulled up into the driveway that led to the complex, Captain Hamlin told me where to put the engine. As soon as I got off the rig, I could hear people screaming from the back of the building. I grabbed a rope bag when I left, and we all started sloshing through the wet grass walking to what I assumed was a small creek.

"I couldn't believe it when I saw this huge river. It was a nasty day out, and it had been raining hard all morning. It was pretty obvious from the time we pulled up that this was not a false alarm. In the middle of this torrent, two girls were hanging on for their lives. It didn't look good for them at all.

"With the speed of the current, they were holding onto tree branches and were lying horizontally in the water. I concentrated on the girl that was closest to us, fourteen-year-old Jennifer Anglin. She was terrified and yelled to me, 'Help me! Help me! I'm going to let go! I can't hang on anymore!'

"I could see there was a lot of debris downstream and if she let go, she would have been carried into it. Becoming tangled in that would have been the end for her. I called out and told her not to give up. 'You've got to hang on. Don't let go.'

"I decided that I was going to tie a rope to me and go in the water and float down to where Jennifer was trapped. There was a large tree on the bank that was just a bit upstream from her. My thinking was to swim out and try to grab her as I went past. Then the rope would wrap around the tree and pull me back to shore. Firefighter McCollum was on the other end of the rope. I had him stand a little downstream of the tree."

Rich did not have any protective gear, such as a life vest or a thermal suit, to protect him from the cold water. Under different circumstances, he might have thrown Jennifer a rope or floated one downstream to her, but fighting the cold water and strong current had taken its toll on the young girl. Even if she were able to grab the rope, it was unlikely that she would have the strength to hold on. If the young girl was going to survive, it would be because a firefighter plucked her from the deadly current.

This was the first time Rich had attempted such a rescue. Throughout the United States, in fire departments large and small, training is a daily ritual. Every conceivable catastrophe is dissected and broken down into a team-concept training program. However, because Santa Rosa is not a river town, the need for a water-rescue training program fell below the radar screen.

"It boiled down to a commonsense approach, as far as what we were going to try. I told McCollum, 'I'll go out in the current and grab her arm, and then the current will probably swing us back into the bank.' It just seemed like a logical plan.

"While we were doing this, Captain Hamlin tried to get the necessary resources, including more ropes and personnel, to respond. No matter what happened to me and Jennifer, we still had another girl in the water."

Jennifer and her friend, fifteen-year-old Marglyn Paseka, had been standing beside the creek watching the water rush past when they noticed some debris floating at the edge of the water. Jennifer reached over and pushed it out so they could watch it float downstream. She lost her footing and fell into the water with Marglyn reaching for her. In an instant both girls were sucked into the torrent. Each of them grabbed onto the branches of small trees as they were being swept downstream. Other people who lived in the apartment complex on the edge of the creek heard the girls' cries for help and came running. When they couldn't reach the girls, the fire department was called.

Rich knew he had to at least make an attempt to get her. "Jennifer was losing confidence in her ability to hold onto the tree. We all were yelling to her not to let go. It was time to go and I got in the water with the rope tied around my waist.

"The water was freezing cold and running very fast. Firefighter McCollum was feeding the rope around the tree to give me some slack. I told Jennifer, 'Don't grab my hand. I am going to get a hold on your forearm.' She nodded in agreement. As I swam farther out, the current picked up until I was where I needed to be and I was coming up on her fast.

"I only had a second to snatch her up as I flew past. She kept her arm where I had a good look at it. At the exact moment, I reached out and clutched with everything I had. It was perfect. I got her, I told her to let go of the tree. She did and just like that, we drifted to the shore. She was safe and so was I. I don't think I spent more than a minute in the water.

"Marglyn was screaming for us to save her as I got to shore with Jennifer. Captain Hamlin came down and helped us out of the water. I handed her off to a police officer. Then, for the first time, I felt really cold from the water. Just then Ladder 1 showed up. They were equipped for a water rescue."

Firefighter Donald Lopez was on the ladder truck. Several months before, he, along with four other firefighters on the Santa Rosa Fire Department, had taken a five-day course in water rescue. Following their training, they pushed for their department to buy the same kind of gear they had used in the class.

"We felt that it was only a matter of time before a situation arose that called for a water rescue. While we don't really have a lot of water, there are times when we get a lot of rain, and creeks that are normally small become big and fast. There was some reluctance to buy the gear, but we prevailed and now the equipment was on the truck. They really weren't against getting the equipment; it was more hesitation because there were so few of us trained in its use. All of the hypothetical situations were now in the past. We had a girl in a raging river and she was going to drown if we didn't get her out. I had the training, and we had the rescue gear, and it was time to put it all to use. But this was going to be my first actual rescue.

"On my way to work that morning, I had stopped by a few creeks to see how high they were. I thought they would be up, but I was surprised at how high they were. When we got the call to Matanzas Creek, I knew we were going to find a dangerous situation. I got to the station and told Captain David Cornelssen about the creeks and suggested that we put the life jackets on the truck just in case. The previous shift had the same idea, and the jackets were already there. When we sat down for lunch that day, we were talking about how high the water was and what we would do if we had to perform a water rescue in one of them.

"We had already heard that the call was a good one before we got there. I was the tillerman on the ladder [steering the back wheels of the very long ladder truck], and as we drove to the call, I knew I was going in the water. I started going over some of the things we had to do as soon as we arrived.

"When we got there, we set up an upstream protection system, which involved placing a firefighter upstream to monitor debris in the water. The last thing you want is a big log or something like it coming down on you while you are trying to rescue someone. Then we set up a downstream recovery system, in case the girl couldn't hold on—or to catch me, for that matter.

"We took all the gear down to the water, and I watched the girl. At that time, I didn't even know Dennis had snatched another girl out of the water. I had heard that there were two people in the water, but I was so focused on the girl in the water I didn't even ask about the other one."

Marglyn Paseka had become hysterical and was obviously petrified. She knew death was breathing down her neck but didn't know what to do. Firefighter McCollum was in the water up to his waist trying to calm her down. He kept up a steady stream of conversation with her. "We're here for you. We are going to help you. Just hold on a little longer."

Captains Cornelssen and Hamlin and Firefighter Lopez were formulating a rescue plan when Lopez saw Marglyn go under the water. "She surfaced and went under again. She was starting to give up. She called out to Greg, 'I can't hold on.' He kept telling her not to give up. It was so important that he was there for her. I don't think she would have lasted if he wasn't talking with her.

"The ideal rescue method is to pull a line from one side to the other at a forty-five-degree angle, have the person in the water grab onto the line, and let the current take them to the opposite bank; or have a rescuer go out attached to the line. That approach wouldn't work in this case because of the thick brush overhead, and we couldn't throw the heavy rope across a creek that was now fifty feet wide. Marglyn told us she was stuck between a tree and a submerged garbage can and said she couldn't free herself."

The crew from Engine 4 had prepared a line that would allow Lopez to enter the water upstream and float down to Marglyn. They planned for him to grab onto the partially submerged tree next to her and effect the rescue. Unlike the situation with Rich, Lopez had a life vest on to keep him afloat.

He wore a "truckman's belt" around his waist, which has a carabineer (a metal ring that allows a rope to be fed through it). By doing this, Lopez was able to control his approach to her. When he got to Marglyn, he was able to stop his descent and remain next to her. If necessary, he could unhook himself and break free. He also carried a length of rope to attach to the girl.

"I got into the water and floated with the current down to where she was, and the firefighters on the line stopped feeding rope out, which kept me in a stationary position next to her. She was in panic mode when I got there. The first thing she told me was that she was going to drown. She said that several times. I was talking with her, trying to calm her down so she could follow directions. I told her she wasn't going to drown and that she would be fine. I am not so sure I believed that, but she didn't need to know how bad I thought things were. She listened to me and seemed somewhat relieved that I was there, but she was still very afraid.

"She told me that her legs were trapped. I felt around to see what was holding her. I could feel one of her feet but not the other. I had hoped that I would be able to use both hands, but the current was so strong that I had to constantly hold onto the tree with one hand and do all of the work with my free hand.

"I was able to move in behind her, so I was protected from the current, which allowed me to work better. I still couldn't find her other foot no matter how much I searched for it. Then suddenly, the current pulled me away from her. She screamed that I was leaving her. I was helpless as the current pushed me away."

As Firefighter Lopez fought to control his position, Firefighter McCollum immediately began a stream of dialog with Marglyn, assuring her they were not leaving her. "Everything is going to be OK. It is just going to take a little longer than we thought, that's all. We aren't going anywhere, and we are going to get you out." Marglyn was starting to lose the small amount of control she had left. Lopez climbed out of the water and ran back upstream, ready to go back in again.

"When I got set to go back in and float down to her and try again, I was given a second belt because the rope didn't work very well. This time, the plan was to secure the belt around her and then to me. That way I could work to free her. When I got down to her, I tried to maneuver into position, but she grabbed me and took me under. She was screaming, 'Don't let me drown! Don't let me drown!'

"She now had me underwater and I had to push her away from me so I could surface again. When I came to the surface, a voice came out of nowhere. 'Marglyn!' It was as if no other sound was present. I looked up on the bank. Dozens of people were up there, but I was focused on only one woman. She was standing up on the slope with tons of people. I had never seen her, but I knew she was Marglyn's mother. She actually took my focus away from the rescue for a moment. I thought to myself, She's going to be all right. We're going to get her. Just relax Mom. Then I returned my focus to Marglyn.

"When I pushed her away from me, I actually moved her to the side of the tree. I still couldn't find her other foot. Without freeing that foot, she wasn't going anywhere. Her hands were still around my neck and I was fighting to keep from going under. If she made me her life jacket, we were both in big trouble."

Lopez was able to wrap his legs around the tree, which gave him much more stability in the strong current. Marglyn was starting to show the effects of hypothermia. As she begged Lopez not to let her drown, her words slurred. From his training, he knew that time was short for her. If she were to lose consciousness in the water, he would not be able to save her alone. By the time a second rescuer could be put in place, it would likely be too late. Then, just as before, he lost his grip on Marglyn and the tree all at once, and was swept downstream.

"I was so frustrated the second time. When I got to the shore Captain Cornelssen came over to me. I told him I was sure I could get her if I could just free her other leg. Captain Hamlin was worried about me and the amount of time I had spent in the water. He told me the Sonoma County Sheriff's Department was ready to lower a man from a helicopter to try the rescue that way."

The truckman's belt Lopez had been using for Marglyn had been an open loop. "My captain hooked the belt ends together to form a closed loop. While the helicopter plan was still being developed, I went back into the water for the third time. The captain's idea with the belt was a good one. I slipped my arm through the belt and it freed one of my hands.

"McCollum was still talking to her from the bank, assuring her we were going to get her out. He was really focused on keeping her head above water. Before I got back to her, she lost her grip and was forced underwater. He yelled at her to bring her focus back on fighting the current. She was able to bend forward and grab the tree again and get her head above water.

"I was face-to-face with her again and told her not to worry—'You're going to be all right.' She said, 'Please don't leave me. Please don't. I know I'm going to drown, but please don't leave me.' I told her she was going to be fine and we were going to have her out in a few minutes. I told her I needed help, but that she was going to be fine. She fired back at me, 'I'm not fine. I'm not going to be fine. I am going to drown.'

"I took the belt and held it out to her. I explained that I was going to slip it over her head, and that I wanted her to put one arm through it and then the other. This got her attention back to me, and away from the understandable panic that had taken control. She would have to let go of the tree for a brief moment to put her arm into the belt. She balked at the idea. I told her that we had to and she wasn't going to go anywhere. I told her to trust me. I said over and over again, 'Everything is going to be fine.'

"She got the belt around her neck and under her arms. Her belt was attached to the same rope I was on. I told her that we had her now and as soon as I was able to free her other foot, we were going ashore.

"The cold was starting to have an effect on me now. I was starting to lose my strength. At that time, I had been in the water for about twenty-five minutes. It was getting harder for me to hold on. It was like my movements were in slow motion. I still couldn't get her free and I didn't understand it.

"I lost my grip on the tree and started to be carried away. As I lunged out to get a hold back on the tree, I heard her scream. In an instant, the rope tightened against her and she was jerked face-first under the water. All I could see were her arms grasping up at the air, searching for something to hold onto that didn't exist. Any sense of safety I felt for her evaporated in a split second. All the assurances to her—that we were going to get her out—seemed very hollow. She was drowning right in front of me as the current pulled me away.

"I thrust my hand out to the rope between us. I don't have a clue how it happened, but I managed to find my strength in a split second and pulled myself back to her. The cold I had felt before was gone. When I pulled myself toward her, she came free, and I held onto her as we drifted to shore. I held her head up, and it was over. We really had saved her."

Cheers broke out from the crowd on the bank and slope by the apartment. As they arrived at the shore, both of them were assisted by firefighters. Marglyn had no strength left as they carried her to the waiting ambulance. Captain Cornelssen came over to Lopez and told him what a fabulous job he had done. The adrenaline rush that supplied Lopez's last surge of strength was gone, and the cold had taken over. He was shaking uncontrollably.

"My captain told me I had to get into the ambulance and go to the hospital. I couldn't stop shaking. I got in the same ambulance with Marglyn. She was in pretty bad shape from the cold, but she thanked me for what we had done. I said to her, 'I told you we'd get you out of there, you just had to believe in us. We were in a bad situation and we were going to get you out, it just took a little longer than we'd expected. You are going to be fine.' She thanked me again. Her mother came to the back of the ambulance and told her that she loved her and that everything would be fine. She looked at me and nodded her head slowly. She smiled at me then and thanked me for saving her girl. McCollum was in the ambulance too. He had spent a long time in the water and was suffering the effects of hypothermia along with us.

"At the hospital, they put us under a hot shower and gave us something warm to drink. Our battalion chief, Owen Wilson, came by to tell us we had done a great job and to relieve us from duty. He told us to go home and relax. After our temperatures came back to normal, we got released."

Back at the fire station, Don Lopez changed into clean clothes. He called his wife, Heidi, and told her he had been released to come home from work. At first she was concerned that something might be wrong. He told her he had been involved in a rescue and was pretty tired. She took it all in stride and asked him to pick up a pizza on the way home.

Lopez was told that his picture was going to be in the paper the following day, which he relayed to his family. His children were excited, and before sunrise the following morning, they burst into his bedroom with the paper. There was photographer Annie Wells's picture of the rescue on the front page of the *Press Democrat*, as well as papers across America. It was a good enough photojournalism shot to win the Pulitzer Prize.

"It is true that I was the one in the water, but there is no way I could have done anything without all the firefighters on the bank such as Rachel Griffith, Gerry Regan, Steve Emerson, Robert Stratton, Captain Robert Hathaway, Clarence Gifford, Ken Sebastiani, Jim Feige, Captain Dave Cornelssen, and Captain Tim Hamlin. Or Greg McCollum, who was standing waist-deep in the water. There was a Petaluma firefighter, Michael Grummell, who was off duty but there holding a rope. I didn't even know him, but he was there for me and Marglyn too. The firefighters on the rope controlled my movement in the water and all of them would have been my support team if something bad happened to me. Sometimes people think that 'team effort' are just words, but while I was in that water, they weren't. I knew I was safe. Not because of my skills, but because of theirs. They allowed me to focus completely on the rescue. I was just one of many."

Donald Lopez and Dennis Rich both received the City of Santa Rosa and the Santa Rosa Fire Department's Medal of Valor and a commendation from the city council for their bravery. They also were given one of *Firehouse* magazine's medals for Heroism and Community Service. They were flown to Kansas City to attend the International Association of Fire Chiefs convention and given the Benjamin Franklin Fire Service Award for Valor (cosponsored by Motorola Corporation). This is the highest award in the world given to a firefighter.

Looking back on the rescue, Don Lopez said, "It was kind of a dream for us both that was fulfilled. We got to rescue somebody. It is what most all firefighters want to do and we got to do it. Neither of us ever imagined all of the awards and things that would come out of it."

14

HER FATHER WAS INSIDE

January 17, 1999

Port Washington, New York

Walter Clark, Geoffrey Cole, Giuseppe "Joe" Sicuranza

January 17, 1999, was a football playoff weekend and a bright, clear day, about thirty degrees outside. At about 12:15 that Sunday afternoon, a call came into the Port Washington Fire Department reporting a house fire at 6 Kirkwood Road with the possibility of people trapped inside.

Fire Inspector Walter Clark was the first to arrive at the scene. He found smoke billowing from the front of the two-story house. "I was at home when the call came in. I only live three blocks from the house, so it didn't take me more than a minute to jump in my car and drive there. I radioed in that we had a working fire so the units would know this one was a good call. Then I opened my trunk and put on my turnout gear and my SCBA. As I walked up to the front of the house, several neighbors were yelling, 'Sonny is still in there! Sonny is trapped!' "

This picture was taken just after the firefighters were evacuated.
The entire first floor exploded in a massive flashover.

Acting on his initial instinct to enter the house and conduct a preliminary search, Clark entered a side door along the driveway side of the house. "When I crawled in, I was on the first floor in the kitchen area. The smoke was banked down to the floor, and it was hot. After determining that the room was clear, I tried to move into the adjoining room, but I couldn't. As hot as the kitchen was, the next room was unbearable. I had full protective gear on, but without a protective hose line, I couldn't go any farther. I was by myself and concerned that I would have to be rescued along with anyone else who was trapped in the house. I was in there no more than five minutes before I decided to try and find another way in.

"When I came out, I was met by a woman who told me that Sonny, her father, was inside, but she didn't know where. I stood back and surveyed the structure. The basement was very involved with fire. The fire was still making its way to the second floor, so based on everything I saw, I decided to go into the basement."

The basement window was to the right side of the front porch. Clark kicked it in, and as he did, thick, black smoke burst forth. Without hesitating, he crawled through the opening and dropped onto the basement floor.

"Once I hit the floor, I lay down to get my bearings. This room was definitely the source of the fire. Smoke was banked down almost to the floor. I couldn't see it, but I could hear the fire above my head. It was eating the first-floor joists and giving off a lot of heat.

"I started to do a left-hand pattern search. I could only see a few inches in front of me, and I ran right into a fuel oil tank. I felt my way around it, moving my hands in an arc in front of me and to the side as I went. Then I felt something. It was Sonny. I touched him, but he didn't respond to me. By this time, the first fire units had arrived. I heard somebody yell out that there was a firefighter in the basement. I called back that I had found Sonny.

"I started to pull him back toward the door, but when I got a grip on him and pulled, he slipped out of my hands. He was so badly burned that his skin pulled off on my gloves. At that time, I called for someone to give me some assistance. I heard another firefighter making his way into the basement through the window I had kicked out."

It was Lieutenant Giuseppe "Joe" Sicuranza. "Our engine pulled out, heading to the call," Sicuranza recalled. "Walter Martinique was driving and [Glenn] Pederson was our captain. I was the lieutenant on the rig, my first call as an officer. Also on the engine were Thomas Cycan and the captain's brother, Roy Pederson.

"As soon as we got there, it was clear we had a serious working fire. Glenn and Roy Pederson advanced an inch-and-three-quarter line into the front door. I was the backup firefighter on the line. We got word that one of our firefighters was in the basement and needed help with a fire victim.

"We left our line and ran down the steps. I was first to the window and went in. Even though it was in the middle of the day, it was pitch-black in the basement. I was screaming for Walter. He told me where he was, and I crawled toward his voice. We both kept yelling for each other, and about a minute later I was with both of them."

The basement was very cluttered, and Sicuranza pushed things out of the way to move the victim toward the window. "I got to the other side of him, and together, Walter and I moved him across the floor. He was completely unconscious, and since he was a big guy, it was tough to move him."

The temperature in the basement continued to climb as the two firefighters worked. The fire victim was in serious trouble. Sicuranza and Clark didn't realize it at that point, but Sonny had second- and third-degree burns over much of his body.

He had been cleaning a propane stove in the basement of his home, doing some remodeling to prepare a room for his daughter, who was coming to live with him. The cleaning solvent he chose was gasoline. At some point the fumes ignited, setting the house on fire.

"When Joe and I got Sonny over to the window," explained Clark, "Joe put a big bear hug on him and lifted him up to the point where Glenn and Roy Pederson were able to reach through and take him. In the process of moving Sonny, I severely hurt my back.

"After Sonny was out, I climbed out the window. All of a sudden, the pain in my back was unbearable. I was taken to the hospital for treatment. Since that day, I have had a bad back. At the time, I didn't have any idea that I had the potential for such a serious injury."

Both firefighters left the basement, which continued to heat up. Conditions were right for a flashover if they were not able to lower the temperature inside the building. At the same time, other units from Port Washington were being put into place to vent the building and attack the fire.

Outside of the house, Assistant Fire Chief Geoffrey Cole heard the disturbing news that children might be trapped on the first floor. He immediately had a line advanced into the house by firefighters from the Protection Engine Company, another fire station in Port Washington, to use as an attack line that would protect them as they performed the search. Using a hose line for protection, the firefighters advanced through the front door and into the living room, beginning an operation that would lead to a search of the first floor.

"At that point, we had very, very heavy smoke conditions on the first floor along with a tremendous amount of heat," said Cole. "The smoke was banked down to within four or five inches of the floor in the hallway. There had already been a search of the second floor. The house was a two-family dwelling, and the fire hadn't invaded the second story."

Engineer Donald Alexander and Firefighters Gary Chudd and Ken Glasser were on the hose line. Alexander was the officer in charge of the line, and as they proceeded down the hallway, conditions began to deteriorate. "When we went in the front door, the smoke was fairly light," reported Alexander. "We made a turn, and we were in the living room. We were looking for the fire. We knew there had been a rescue out of the basement and that the fire had originated there.

"As we made our way down the hall, the smoke went down to the floor, and the heat was extremely high. Chudd was the nozzle man, and Ken was the backup on the hose. So far, we hadn't seen any visual evidence of fire. As we got deep into the hall, it was pitch-black and there was no evidence of daylight, only thick smoke.

"We got to a door in the hallway that appeared to lead to the basement. I told my crew to stop for a moment. I could see a red glow around
the frame of the door and heavy smoke coming out from the bottom. If
we were going to really attack this fire successfully, we had to get to its
base, which was in the basement. I know how intimidating it can be to
advance a line into a basement filled with fire, and I wanted to prepare
them for what we were going to confront.

"My body was facing ahead, and I turned around to talk to them
when it happened. Flames came through the door and it just disintegrated. Flames rolled over the top of us. I told Chudd to open the nozzle and play the water on the ceiling and keep the flames off of us.

"But this fire was different from anything I had seen before. It was
red like I would expect, but it had blue mixed in with it. I thought there
had to be something, perhaps propane, accelerating this fire because it
was burning just too hot. Rarely do you see a blue flame with a wood
structure fire. I was right, we had propane feeding the blaze. When the
fire rolled over the top of us, Gary moved so quickly that his helmet and
facepiece became dislodged."

Assistant Chief Cole was behind the three firefighters and watched
the fireball come from the basement and down the hall. He yelled out a
warning that the floor was getting ready to flash over. The crew that
searched the second floor had come back down and was conducting the
first-floor search. They were close to the side door and were either on
their hands and knees or stomachs to try and escape from the heat. The
searching crew went out the side door.

"When I saw the flames overtake the crew, I moved forward to help.
When Chudd lost the protection of his facepiece, he released his grip on
the hose as he tried to reposition his gear. I moved in to take up the hose
and try and cool off the hallway and give protection to them so we could
retreat.

"With the amount of heat in that area of the house and the way the
flames came over them, I felt we had a real threat of a general flashover
that could take the lives of all of us," said Cole. "I didn't know it then,
but the basement door was a very thin luan mahogany type [a wood cov-

ering for inexpensive side doors]. It was amazing that it held the fire as long as it did. The nozzle was partially open, so I positioned it to get the maximum amount of water. It was critical to cool down the burning gases to give us time to get out.

"I told them to get out now. I pushed them back with one hand and held the hose with the other. I couldn't turn off the water. If I did, the fire would have been all over us. As I got to the door, I just dropped the hose. I didn't even shut it off. The firefighters at the front door grabbed me and pulled me down the stairs. When I got to the bottom, the house exploded into fire."

The exact moment was captured on film. Burning debris flew through the air, and molten vinyl siding fell as a terrifying rain on the firefighters outside. Two of the three men from Protection Engine Company were burned. Alexander and Chudd both suffered burns to their faces, but fortunately, they were not serious. Following treatment at a local hospital, they returned to regular duty. The information about the possibility of children being trapped inside was erroneous. Emergency medical technician (EMT) Lieutenant Christina Marvullo was also working the fire. She watched as her fiancé, Alexander, was transported by ambulance from the scene. She later reflected that not knowing the extent of his injuries and still performing her job at the fire was very difficult.

Sonny's daughter wrote a letter to the Port Washington Fire Department thanking them for their brave actions that day and the gift they had bestowed upon her. She said she spent five days with her father at the hospital before he died of his injuries. She had those days because of the brave firefighters who risked their own safety for her father. Although he died, they had returned him to her. Even though it was for only for a brief period of time, it was a gift.

For their selfless action in defense of others, Assistant Chief Geoffrey Cole, Fire Inspector Walter Clark, and Firefighter Giuseppe Sicuranza were awarded medals for their heroic actions by *Firehouse* magazine as part of their Heroism and Community Service program. They also received the Nassau County Gold Medal of Valor. They each received the Medal of Valor from their own department as well. Chief Cole was awarded the Texaco Life Saving Award, one of only a hundred given since 1902.

To this day, Donald Alexander's helmet is on display at the fire department. It is encrusted with the molten vinyl that dripped from the house, and it gives silent testimony to its protective quality. He is now a captain and routinely gives training to young firefighters. "I tell them that on January 17, 1999, I didn't have my Nomex hood properly placed, and I got burned. It was a valuable lesson—one of many that day."

Cole doesn't know how he summoned the strength to push and guide the firefighters with one hand and play the hose back and forth on the flames with the other, buying them all precious seconds. He looks with pride at the young men he helped that midwinter afternoon. "Two of those guys have since gotten married and had children. It is nice to see the product of that rescue."

When asked about that day in the hallway, one of the firefighters said, "We are here today because of the chief. It is that simple."

15

CELEBRATING THE FOURTH

July 4, 1998

Los Angeles County, California

Ron McFadden

A sign on Highway 138 in Southern California's upper desert area reads "Stay Alert, Stay Alive." The highway has been the scene of some grisly automobile crashes, and Ron McFadden's Los Angeles County Fire Department Engine 79 was no stranger to the carnage.

It was the Fourth of July, 1998, and Vicky Lister and her cousin Mary Goodley were traveling to visit family. Vicky's nine-year-old daughter, Shanika, was in the backseat. As Vicky's car approached the bridge over the California Aqueduct, another vehicle attempted an unsafe pass, which caused the two cars to go off the road to avoid a head-on collision. One of them made it back on the road, but Vicky Lister lost control of her car. After leaving the roadway, her car tore through a chain-link fence and was launched into the air. Flying at least seventy-five feet, it landed in an eighteen-foot-deep canal, one of the main

Ron McFadden, Los Angeles County Fire Department.

drinking-water sources for the Los Angeles basin. The car immediately filled with water, turned over, and sank to the bottom.

A motorist who witnessed the accident noticed that the driver of the car who caused the accident did not stop. He gave chase, and the car was eventually stopped. The driver was arrested and charged with reckless driving and leaving the scene of an accident.

Witnesses to the accident with cellular telephones immediately called the Los Angeles County Fire Department to report the incident. At Fire Station 79, the call came in as "Water rescue, 79's area, Highway 138 at 228 Street East; vehicle in the aqueduct with people trapped inside."

As the car settled to the bottom, Vicky Lister covered her mouth with her hand. "My first reaction was panic. I couldn't swim, and I knew I couldn't drink all that water. I thought I was going to choke. The Lord allowed me to see the light above so I could find my way to the surface." Vicky felt that if she could get to the surface she could call for help and made her way out of the driver's door window. Mary did the same on the passenger's side. Several people who saw the accident stopped their cars and looked into the water as Vicky came up.

"When I got up to the surface, I began yelling for help. I had seen television shows where someone needed help and bystanders came to their aid, but that didn't happen. They all just looked at me. I told them my daughter was trapped and I couldn't swim."

Her call to help her daughter was heard by one of the bystanders, who immediately dove into the water. Vicky and Mary made their way to the side of the canal and held on to keep themselves afloat. The good Samaritan dove down over and over again, attempting in vain to find the car.

While this was happening, Gary McAdam was the first one out of Station 79 in his fire patrol truck. The patrol vehicle is used in the high desert area where a large engine cannot travel. Engine 79 was right behind. When McAdam arrived at the scene, he saw no sign of the car. Firefighter Paramedics Jim LaRue and Jeff Britton, from Squad 92, were also en route in an advanced life support unit.

By now, Shanika had been trapped underwater for about eighteen minutes, so she was no longer breathing.

The engine arrived with Captain Mark Hanson, Firefighter Specialist Ron McFadden, and Firefighter Mike Will. McFadden ran to the edge of the canal and saw the man who was trying to find the car without success.

"Though he hadn't found the car, he was a great help nonetheless. At least we knew where the car wasn't. As I stood there, Jeff Britton walked up to me.

"He said, 'The SCBA air mask would work.' Then he told me about his military training where they talked about the SCBA being a descendant of the system used by divers. He went on to say they were good to a depth of about thirty-five feet. I am a certified diver myself, and I remembered training where we had to take off our masks and air tanks and breathe directly from the bottle.

"I grabbed an SCBA. I knew I was going in the water. I was the most highly trained water-rescue firefighter at the scene and I thought no matter what, I was better off with it then without it.

"I listened to Jeff Britton tell me about the SCBA, but he wasn't all that convincing when he told me the story. I asked him if he was sure that it would work, and he said he was. So I put it on, tightened my faceplate really well, and got ready to go in the water. I had to make sure that it would work one more time.

"With my facepiece in place, I put both my hands on Jeff Britton's shoulders and asked him one more time, 'Now this is something you've done before, right? You didn't just read about it in a magazine or anything like that, did you?' He shook his head no. Looking back, I wonder which question he was answering.

"I was going to give it a try, and if it didn't work, I planned to remove the faceplate and just breathe the air directly out of the tube. Before I went into the water, Firefighter Mike Will secured a rope to the back of my SCBA tank. This was going to be my safety line if I got into any trouble.

"I got in the water and told myself to calm down. I was not at all convinced that it would work. The little girl had been underwater for about thirty minutes by now. If I had really thought about it, I would have said this was not a rescue operation, it was a body recovery. That is one of the heartbreaking things about this job. You set yourself up for failure and to be let down all the time. You are constantly trying to beat odds that can't be beaten, but we try anyway—every day."

The water in the California Aqueduct will eventually be treated and become drinking water, but where it crosses under the Pearblossom Highway, it looks more suitable for frogs. It was a green and murky mess. As McFadden made his first dive to the bottom, it was a total failure. Instead of descending, he unknowingly swam in an eight-foot circle and never got much below the surface.

"The first try was pretty much a bust, but I realized what I was doing wrong and tried again. This time I forced myself to the bottom and went in a circle on the bottom. As soon as I went under, the system that checks the flow of air failed and my air began to flow at a full rate. Normally, you just get air when you draw a breath, but not underwater. There are a lot of catfish in that water, and I expected to run my hand into the muck on the bottom and come back with a fish firmly attached to it.

"Then something I hadn't counted on occurred: my low-air alarm went off. This meant I had five minutes of air left, but that was at a normal flow. This was certainly a negative turn of events, but no sooner than that happened when I touched something. I had found the car."

Vicky Lister watched as McFadden searched frantically. Once the firefighters arrived and he went in the water, she felt an inner peace come over her. "I knew Ron would find her. He wasn't going to give up." She prayed for him to have the strength and courage to find her little girl. She hadn't considered that humans can't survive thirty-five minutes with no air. To her, the firefighters were angels sent from God to spare her Shanika.

McFadden was on the bottom, trying to find an entrance to the car. "I didn't really know if she was even still in the car at that point. She could have been ejected and not come to the surface. Luckily, the window on the side of the car I was on was broken out. The car was upside down and resting on the concrete bottom of the canal.

"When I found the window, I reached in. In my mind I had envisioned that when I found the car, if the little girl were still inside, I could simply reach inside, undo her seat belt, and pull her out. I reached inside and found her, but she was in the middle seat, and while I could touch her, I wasn't able to undo her belt. So I swam inside. Shanika was lifeless and still fastened in her seat belt. I undid her belt, and she began to float. I had to pull her down to get her out of the window. Then I swam about seventeen feet to the surface. As I reached the top, I ran out of air and had to pull my mask off so I could breathe."

Vicki's eyes opened wide in amazement as she watched the water begin to churn. "I couldn't believe it when Ron McFadden came to the surface, the water was swirling all around. It was like a waterfall and the water wasn't green. It was the whitest I had ever seen. He shot out of the water like a dolphin, and she was under his arm. I prayed out loud, 'Thank you Jesus for this miracle, but please finish it and bring her back.' "

On the surface, Firefighter McFadden handed the lifeless girl to Firefighter Paramedics Britton and LaRue. Shanika Lister was not breathing and was in full cardiac arrest. She had been underwater for about forty-five minutes. On their hands and knees, they started from zero with the little girl. A few feet away, her mother also knelt in the dirt, praying for a miracle that did not seem to be happening. Nearby in the water, McFadden was spent, unable to help himself. McAdams saw him and alerted others to come to his aid. It was time to rescue the rescuer and make sure he was able to get out of the water. Then, with the help of the paramedics, McAdams began CPR on Shanika.

A Los Angeles County Fire Department helicopter had been dispatched when the original call came out, and it had already arrived. Shanika was quickly put onboard, and as they took off, McAdams continued to perform CPR.

Sometimes you can pump and breathe for all you are worth and you still can't bridge the gap. Most of the time you can't reach into the shadow of death and pull a person back into the sunlight of the living. I know. I have tried and failed many times.

As the chopper disappeared into the desert sky, it was very quiet at the rescue site. Everyone had done his best, now it was time to wait and see. McFadden felt no certainty about the safety of Shanika, as the little girl had no visible spark of life. Another call came a few minutes later. Engine 79 was off again, this time to rescue a group of stranded hikers.

About four hours later, the firefighters returned to the station and saw McAdams, who told them about the little girl. By the time the helicopter arrived at the hospital, he had finished his CPR efforts. Just before they landed, Shanika's heart began to beat again, and she started breathing. Shanika Lister was in critical condition, but she was alive. To her mother, it was quite simple. "Every one of those firefighters sent to the canal that day was an angel assigned from God."

Ron McFadden was given the Los Angeles Fire Department's Medal of Valor for rescuing little Shanika Lister. He had done something no other firefighter had done in the memory of his superiors when he entered the water with a SCBA and used it in such a manner. Later it was determined that he only had about two minutes of air when he dove down into the murky waters searching for a life. Had he become lodged in the car, his life might well have ended. He didn't know that his air supply was to end in less than thirty seconds when he crawled in through the window of the car. Sometimes what you don't know can help save your life or in that case, another's.

It has been a long road back, but Shanika made the journey. She has returned to school and while she has lost some of her motor skills, she is recovering. To Vicky, every breath Shanika takes is a gift from God— as were the angels sent that fateful day where Pearblossom Highway crosses over the California Aqueduct. Vicky and her little girl found a new reason to celebrate the Fourth of July.

16

THE DAY THE SUN LOST ITS RADIANCE

July 9, 2001

Chewuch River Valley, Washington

Tom Craven, Karen FitzPatrick, Jessica Johnson, Devin Weaver, Rebecca Welch

Summertime in Washington State's Wenatchee National Forest is a busy place. Campers come to enjoy all that the mountains, meadows, and water have to offer. Most of the time, things go smoothly. The rules are simple: clean up after yourself, camp in designated places, have safe campfires, and always put them completely out. But rules were made to be broken, and in July of 2001, unextinguished coals at a campsite turned into a major conflagration that became known as the Thirty-Mile Fire.

At 9:26 P.M. on July 9, a fire was reported to Okanogan Fire Dispatch. Two hours later, forest fire–fighting crews had been alerted and had arrived on the scene.

Clockwise from top left: Tom Craven, Karen FitzPatrick, Jessica Johnson, Rebecca Welch, and Devin Weaver of the United States Forestry Service.

Tom Craven was at home that evening. He had been notified of the blaze and knew it was only a matter of time before he and his crew would be called into action. He went to bed at eleven o'clock that evening, but forty-five minutes later his wife, Evelyn, woke him. The call had come. He was an experienced wildlands firefighter and would be leading his crew against the monster he loved to tame. It was the kind of challenge that excited him.

Evelyn made sure Tom had all the things he needed for the pack he carried on these assignments. As he sat on the couch watching television, waiting to go to the Perkins Restaurant and Bakery to be picked up by his crew, she told him that she was going to bed. "I always said the same thing to Tom when he went out to fight a fire. I said to him, 'Honey, I'm going to bed. You come back to me safe.' Tom looked at me and said, 'I'll be fine.' Every fire was the same with us. I always said the same thing to him."

Tom Craven's crew was part of a twenty-one-person group known as Northwest Regulars Number Six (NWR #6). This group was headed up by Ellreese Daniels, who had twenty-one years of firefighting experience, and Pete Kampen, who was also an experienced firefighter training to become a crew chief. Craven was in charge of Squad Three of NWR #6, which included Rebecca Welch, a rookie firefighter. Earlier in the day, she had been told that they would be dispatched later that night to Winthrop, Washington, to fight the large South Libby Fire. This was only her second fire. At this point, there had been no discussion of NWR #6 going to the Thirty-Mile fire.

Karen FitzPatrick, Devin Weaver, and Emily Hinson also got the call to be ready to go that night. They were all rookies on their way to the first really big fire they had seen. For some of them, it was their first fire of any size.

FitzPatrick, only eighteen years old, had graduated from high school a month earlier and just passed her forestry service tests. This was a summer job for other rookies, but for FitzPatrick, it was training; she wanted a career as a firefighter.

Hinson was going to her first fire. She was also eighteen and had just joined the fire service. She was on her way to college in the fall, and this was a summer job that was interesting as well as challenging. She lived only two hundred yards from the Leavenworth Ranger Station. When the call to respond came in, she just grabbed her pack and walked over.

At age nineteen, Jessica Johnson had just finished her second year of college. This was her second year in the fire service, and she was assigned to NWR #6. Johnson lived in the forestry service barracks, and when she heard they were to be dispatched that night, she called home and left a message on the answering machine to let her family know she was heading out.

When wildlands firefighters leave, they must carry enough clothing for two weeks. Barbara Weaver made sure her son Devin had the socks he told her he needed. He also brought along a new lunch pail filled with freshly made sandwiches. He was twenty-one and his forestry service job represented college money.

Twenty-one-year-old Jason Emhoff, a squad boss trainee, was also part of NWR #6. This was his third year of firefighting, and Karen Fitz-Patrick was on his squad. When he had first started fighting wildlands fires it was just a fun and sometimes exciting job. But by the time the Thirty-Mile Fire broke out, he knew he wanted to be a career firefighter.

All of them headed out to do what they had trained for and loved— fighting fires. Excitement was in the air; they were off to fight a big fire. When the sun came up that morning, they didn't know that four of them would not see it set. Tom Craven, Karen FitzPatrick, Jessica Johnson, and Devin Weaver would be burned to death in a picturesque place called the Chewuch River Valley by what became known as the Thirty-Mile Fire.

When the twenty-one crew members of NWR #6 reached their staging area, they got some bad news. They would not be heading to the big fire. Instead they were being sent to a small fire near the Thirty-Mile campground.

Rebecca Welch got out of the van at the Twisp Ranger Station. Her squad boss was Tom Craven, which was fine with her. He was an experienced firefighter who made her feel safe.

"Whenever you worked with Tom, you had fun. He knew the difference between those serious times and periods where joking around was appropriate. I felt good to be working for him. In fact, it seemed more like you were working *with* him, because he could lead without being overbearing. He never stressed you out. He told you what he needed from you, and if you didn't understand, he would show you. All of us really liked him.

"We were told we were going to tightline the fire, which meant we would be digging our lines up close to the fire so it wouldn't get beyond us. We started marching toward one of the spot fires, small ones created from the flying embers coming off of the main blaze. We came to the Chewuch River and crossed it by walking across downed trees. Finally, we got to the fire and started digging a line around it. I used a combination tool that had a shovel as well as prongs for pulling up roots.

"Oh my God, it was hot. There were times we had to turn away from the flames because the heat was so intense. I worked a few feet away from Karen FitzPatrick. It was only about eleven in the morning, and it was supposed to be hot that day. But it was really hot where we were.

"There was another crew that was part of NWR #6, led by Thom Taylor, cutting lines on the same fire. They were working on the other side, and eventually, we met up with each other. And still another crew was attempting to put water on the fire, but they were having a lot of trouble because the hose kept breaking. Emhoff said we had to get water on the fire if we were going to have any chance to control it.

"Emhoff and Craven walked along the line making sure it held. They thought it looked good, and then it happened. The fire crowned and jumped the line by going from one treetop to another. We had people like Devin Weaver, who was cutting brush on the line, trying to prevent this from happening. They were working as hard as they could, but it didn't work. All our efforts to contain that spot fire failed and we had to pull back."

When the fire jumped the line, it was time to retreat to a previously designated safety zone. Welch remembers, "We relieved the Entiat Hot Shots that morning and were trying to hold the lines they had cut during the night. They were the crew that had been the first to fight the fire the night before. They were back at a safety zone, sleeping. The plan was to awaken them at 3:30 in the afternoon, and they would relieve us.

"What we really needed was water. We did have two five-hundred-gallon trucks come in. They put a total of eight hundred gallons on the fire, but it was just too little. They left with one hundred gallons in reserve each, in case they got trapped and had to protect themselves."

It was hard to know what was actually going on for the rookies who were on their very first fires. Hinson and FitzPatrick were both experiencing their first fires. They had been told to trust their crew bosses as well as the firefighters in charge of the squads to which they were assigned, and they did.

Hinson and her crew pulled back to the lunch spot, where they watched the fire as it burned nearby. New spot fires were reported, and the crew moved back to the road and were transported in a van driven by Pete Kampen to cut lines around the new small fires.

"We were out of the van and without any warning, we heard a roaring sound and a wall of flames about fifty feet high burst out at us. Pete Kampen yelled for us to all get into the van. This was not anything I had ever seen before and I was scared.

"We all got in and shut the doors. Kampen was very cool; he started up the van and began heading down the dirt road. We didn't go very far when the flames crossed the road in front of us. He never even slowed down and drove right into them.

"All you could see was red everywhere. The heat from the fire was coming through the glass and we had to lean away to protect ourselves. Flames were curling right over the top of us. I didn't think that anybody left on the road behind us was going to get out."

Kampen was on the radio talking with Daniels. He told him the flames had crossed the road, but they had made it through. Daniels didn't realize it yet, but he and the thirteen other firefighters deeper in the canyon were trapped. They were about to be tested in a way more terrible than any of them could imagine.

They were firefighters, every one, some new and some experienced, but nonetheless firefighters all. When word came from Kampen that he had pulled out, Ellreese Daniels made the decision to move to a safer place. Their van was a ten-passenger model, and they had fourteen men and women along with their gear. Thom Taylor was driving the van with Daniels in the front passenger seat. They proceeded slowly down the road with Craven, Firefighter Beau Clarke, Emhoff, and Welch jogging down the road after them.

Emhoff joked that this was one of the reasons they all trained—so they could run from fires. Neither he nor Craven was concerned; this was part of firefighting. When the place you were in got dangerous, you moved. The spot fire they had been sent to take care of had been no more than an acre, but that was then. Now it was much larger. Welch was glad they were not worried. It must mean that everything was all right.

"I was a little concerned when we came around a corner and the van had stopped ahead of us," Welch remembers. "They were turning around, and there was a wall of fire that had crossed the road, cutting off our escape. When the van came back, we were told to get in. We all just piled in and off we went. Jessica Johnson said to me, 'God, that was close.' I agreed. I had never wanted to get that close to any fire.

"When we went up to the spot fire, Tom Craven pointed out our safety zones and where our escape routes were located. Now the fire had consumed all of them. But we were heading up the road, and I thought we would find a way out farther up the canyon. I didn't know we were driving up a dead-end road in a canyon that was going to be totally filled with fire in a very short amount of time."

As the van drove along, Daniels studied the area. He looked around and said to Taylor, "Stop. Stop." Then a moment later he said, "No, no, no, keep going." The van took off again. This happened a few times, and then Daniels found the place he was looking for and again told Taylor to stop. All of them got out of the van and they discussed where they could deploy if the fire overcame them. On one side of the road, a river was below them, and on the other they had a rock scree (field) area that contained large boulders and other rocks, perhaps a foot in diameter. And then they considered the road they were parked on, which to Welch looked like a safe place to wait out the fire.

"It was about four in the afternoon, and the fire seemed long gone. You couldn't see it, taste it, or feel it. Jessica Johnson and I went up and sat on one of a series of large rocks. She said something that really surprised me. She said, 'We should mentally deploy our shelters, go over the whole thing in our heads.' I was quite shocked and said, 'Are you serious? Do you think we will have to do that?' She said, 'Maybe.'

"That was when I started getting scared. Everyone else was just talking as though nothing was wrong. On this huge rock, Tom Craven, Jason Emhoff, and Devin Weaver were all talking. Jason Emhoff could see that I was scared and he called me over to talk to me."

"This was Rebecca's first fire and I could tell she was getting pretty concerned about everything so I called to her," Emhoff remembers. "I told her everything was going be OK. At that point I didn't feel we were going to be in any imminent danger. It isn't unusual to have a fire go through an area. You wait it out, then move through after it is gone.

"Tom Craven was something else. If there was anything he loved to do, it was to teach firefighters about their trade. He was holding an impromptu class on fire behavior. He was pointing out the characteristics of smoke columns and what they tell about the fire."

A truck with a camper on the back drove up to where the van was parked and two civilians jumped out. Somehow, they were unaware that a fire was in the canyon. Welch looked over, but didn't speak with them. She was more concerned with what Craven had to say.

"On the rocks above the road, Tom finished talking, and we were all looking at the smoke columns and taking pictures of them. Most of us carried disposable cameras to take pictures of the fire. The pictures were good souvenirs and we used them for training as well. Ellreese Daniels went over to the campers and asked them where the road led. We then learned it was a dead end. Then you could see that the fire was beginning to come closer to us. We were just praying it wouldn't overtake us. I guess some prayers don't get answered.

"Thom Taylor said he was going to check out the spot fire that was closest to us. He walked up through the rock scree to get a better look at it. He was quite a bit up the slope from the road. Ellreese kept telling everyone over and over to keep calm."

Welch's mind was going very fast. She tried to think of what she would do if the fire came. "I was trying to figure out what the hell was going on. I had been trained in deploying my shelter, but this was for real, which was quite different. The road seemed like the best place to be if I had to get in my shelter."

A fire shelter is a paper-thin aluminum and fiberglass film that firefighters pull over themselves as a last-ditch defense against flames. To use the shelter, firefighters remove the carrying pouch from their belts and open up the shelter. It is similar to a cocoon that is open on one side (this is the side that will face the ground when the firefighter lies down in the shelter). The bottom of the shelter is stepped into and the top pulled over the head. Then the firefighter lies down and pulls the sides of the shelter inward, which seals it to the ground.

The film is designed to reflect heat without retaining any, while trapping breathable air inside. It will withstand about 1,200 degrees, but wildlands fires are frequently at least 1,600 degrees. At this writing, 1,050 deployments of these shelters have occurred, and all but twenty-four firefighters survived.

Karen FitzPatrick joined the group on the rock. Emhoff and Craven were having a conversation about their respective music favorites. While they were talking, FitzPatrick wrapped her arm around Emhoff's leg. She was frightened. Then the sky opened up. Down on the road, Rebecca Welch was elated to see the rain.

"It was so hot and dry that day. Everyone had been saying how much we needed rain. Now, holy cow, it's raining. It's five o'clock and it's raining, so now maybe the fire will calm down.

"Then I realized what the rain was—fire. A blast of hot air carried the swirling mass of embers. In the background was the sound of an approaching freight train. There was no rain. There was not going to be any settling down of the blaze. It was in full force and it was on top of us. 'Deploy, deploy, deploy, deploy, deploy,' Ellreese Daniels yelled. This really was it."

The campers were in trouble; they had no protection. The burning embers were in their hair and on their clothes, and they were in an absolute state of panic. The eight firefighters on the road unpacked their shelters and prepared to get into them, but the campers had no shelters.

Up on the rock, the embers came with a rush of very hot air. Emhoff and Craven remained relaxed and tried to calm down the firefighters with them. Emhoff had seen ember showers before. "You just huddle very close together and wipe them away off each other. That worked at first, but then the fire was on top of us. Thom Taylor was still on the slope above us and could see what was happening as the fire overtook us.

"Karen FitzPatrick, Devin Weaver, Jessica Johnson, Tom Craven, and I all stood up. It was our intention to go to the road, but we couldn't make it. It was too hot and the flames were coming. Our only hope was to go up the slope and either outrun it or deploy in the rocks."

On the road, Ellreese Daniels helped Welch open her fire shelter. The firefighters told each other to remain calm as they worked to deploy their shelters. Welch pulled her fire gloves on tight as Ellreese opened her shelter up.

"Ellreese gave me the shelter after he opened it. The two campers were standing right next to me. They were freaking out. The embers were burning them. I was scared to death, but at least I had training. They had nothing.

"They didn't have hats on and their hair was full of burning embers. I had a hard hat on, which shielded me from the rain of fire. At that time we were only seconds away from being overrun. I looked at them as I was getting into my shelter and they were pleading for help. That was it. I knew my one-person fire shelter was going to have to be a home for three.

"There was no way I could get into it as it was intended, not with everyone. I had a big problem in that I had no idea how this was going to work out, let alone teach them what to do. I knew that the shelter had to be sealed to the ground to have a chance to make it.

"I told them, 'This is what we have to do. We have to stay calm. We have to hold [the shelter] down to the ground so the wind from the fire doesn't lift it up. The shelter has to stay on top of us, don't pull on it, just hold it down with your hands. We all have to do our part, and hold down this shelter.' I left the part out that we would all die if we didn't do it right, but I was sure we were all thinking that. And when the fire came, we were all curled up under that little silver blanket."

The five firefighters up on the rocks tried to make it down to the road, but were cut off by the fire and heat. When that failed, they tried to outrun the conflagration. It didn't work. The fire came in the form of two funnel clouds, twisting and turning in an unpredictable path. And now those paths were going to cross. Taylor yelled for them to get into their shelters. Emhoff realized for the first time that he had left his fire gloves in the van. He pulled the package containing his shelter from its pouch.

"I was thinking that this was really it. We weren't practicing anymore. I had trained several times getting into a shelter, but now everything was on the line. I kept trying to think ahead and consider a plan for survival.

"Tom reassured everyone that everything was going to be all right. It was so Tom, teaching every minute. It is so impossible to think how all our lives were going to change in the next minute. I watched Devin Weaver and Karen FitzPatrick get into their shelters. It was impressive how fast they did it and correctly too.

"Jessica Johnson was closest to me. She got into her shelter before I did. When I pulled my shelter on and lay down I accidentally kicked her in the head and she yelled out. We were all talking to each other to make sure we were all set. Then a deafening roar came and with it a wave of heat I had never felt before. Everyone has burned their hands on a hot pot or something; this was that same feeling only it was everywhere on my body. I hurt so much. Above us, Thom Taylor was in his shelter, but he couldn't seal it down because of the rocks.

"I was in trouble right away. Embers flew around under my shelter, and my hands were burning. I wasn't talking anymore, but what I heard still echoes in my heart. Karen started to pray. I am sure we could all hear her. Then Jessica prayed too.

"Thom Taylor knew he was dead if he stayed in his shelter. I have no idea how he was able to do what he did, but he jumped up and using his shelter as a shield, he ran down the rock slope and dove in the river. This would have been a tricky maneuver at any time, let alone in the middle of a fire. Thom always wore a hooded Nomex shirt and took a lot of kidding for that when no one else took that extra precaution. It became a brilliant move on his part as he ran for his life.

"The temperature inside my shelter was way up, and I was having a hard time breathing. I thought that maybe if I just held my breath and closed my eyes and slept for a little bit, everything would be all right," Emhoff remembers. "I could just wake up in an hour or so. Then I heard Devin Weaver cry out, 'I'm burning.'

"No, I couldn't do what I was going to do. I couldn't, because if I held my breath, it would be my last one. When Devin cried out, things became clearer for me. I made it this far, I couldn't give up. I yelled out, 'This is too much, I'm leaving.' No one answered.

"I stood up and there was fire everywhere. I saw the fire shelters of Tom, Karen, Jessica, and Devin. There was no movement, and I knew they were gone."

Under Welch's shelter, things were still very challenging. Her crash course in fire shelter etiquette had accomplished its goal. But now the campers were thinking about leaving the shelter.

"They had a million questions. I just wanted them to be quiet and conserve the oxygen we had. But they were very scared; I was too. I was responsible for them, and I had to make sure we all got out of there.

"I searched my mind for what to do next. Then the answer came to me. 'Our Father who art in heaven.' I started to pray and then all of us recited the Lord's Prayer, over and over.

"That calmed them down for a time. Then one of them started hyperventilating and said she couldn't breathe. I told her she had to stop talking [but that she should] put her face to the ground and inhale the dirt if she wanted to. She did. It was strange. I don't know where my composure came from.

"Then one of them got claustrophobic and wanted to get out of the shelter. That would have been the end of all of us. I didn't realize I remembered all the things I had been taught. Now the things my instructors said to me, I had been saying to them.

"It was hot inside the shelter, but not unbearably so. I knew I was burned on my right side by that point, but I also knew that no matter what it was like inside, it was a lot worse on the outside. I said, 'What are you doing? Don't go out there. Don't get out.' Then up went a corner of the shelter. I yelled to pull it back down. And that took care of the problem. It was a good thing they couldn't read my mind, because I wasn't thinking kind thoughts about either of them."

For Emhoff, his only chance at life was to do the unthinkable and leave the shelter. This violated the most basic rule of fire-shelter deployment, but every rule has an exception and this was one of them. He ran to some large boulders and sought shelter from the fire and heat.

"I was trying to find a safe point, but the rocks were not it. There was fire everywhere. I got up from there and ran up the hill. That didn't work either. My time was running out. The heat was taking its toll. I thought if I fell down, I might not get back up again. I looked down at my hands. They were melting. The skin was hanging off. I always wore a lucky bracelet on my wrist and it was melted into my skin.

"The trees were all on fire, the downed ones were burning too. Some of the rocks had split from the heat. Then I got the answer. I saw the van on the road and it wasn't burned up.

"I put everything I had into making it to the road. I kept thinking that inside the van I would be all right. Thom Taylor was calling everyone to come to the river. I wasn't going to go to there because I thought I might go into shock with the cold water and my burns. I wasn't sure what all was burned, but I knew it was a lot.

"I got to the truck and I opened the door. The handles were several hundred degrees, but it didn't matter by then. I got in and closed the door, but it was much too hot inside so I cracked the door. When I did, hot embers began blowing in on me. I was so tired I couldn't even wipe them off and they burned me. I didn't care, I just stayed there."

When the call came to go to the river, Welch was ready to leave the shelter. She and the campers climbed out and made their way to the water. Unquestionably, she was dressed better for the fire than her shelter mates. A burning log lay between them and the river, and one of the campers burned her hand when she put it on the log to climb over it. Once in the river, they submerged themselves and kept their shelters over their heads. The time for burning flesh had passed, and the heartaches had just begun.

At 5:38, a roll call confirmed what Emhoff already knew. Tom Craven, Karen FitzPatrick, Jessica Johnson, and Devin Weaver had died.

A forestry service truck pulled up to the FitzPatrick home at 2:45 A.M. After the truck left, John and Kathie, Karen's mom and dad, sat in the dark kitchen and cried. When the sun came up to a different world, Kathie went into the garden and picked a small bouquet of tiger lilies and put it on the kitchen table next to a picture of her lost girl. Later would come countless letters and tributes from very diverse people and groups, extolling the virtues of a beautiful young woman whose Christian conviction was solid. She was a person who really cared about others.

When Jessica's mother, Jody Gray, heard the sound of a diesel engine, she went to the door. "As soon as I saw the forest service uniforms, I screamed. I knew something had happened to my Jessica." Later she would write a poem eulogizing her lost girl saying, "The sun has lost its radiance now that you are in heaven."

Jessica's father, Rick Johnson, got a telephone call that night from Jody relaying the terrible news. The next day, as he sat with his head in his hands, the words came to him in the form of a poem he read at Jessica's funeral. "My angel then and now. My light of my life now darkened. My joy and my sorrow. My little girl. My grown woman. My helper. My confidante. My ambassador of cheer, laughter, and kindness. My admirer. My girl with the beautiful smile. My hero. My daughter."

In reflection, he said he always tried to instill in Jessica a spirit of adventure and added, "I have thought about this and I think that in some way I may have contributed to her demise."

There was no personal visit to Ken and Barbara Weaver. At one the following morning, a telephone call came. "There has been an incident and Devin has been killed." Devin's mother stated simply, "This has torn our lives apart. It is impossible to think of him as deceased. In my mind, he has gone off somewhere. I remember how excited he was to be going to fight a big fire. When he stood at the door I said, 'Have fun and be careful.' And then he was gone. He was such a fine young man."

Tom Craven's wife, Evelyn, was watching the news that evening when she learned of missing firefighters. She was concerned because they referred to the Entiat Hot Shots and Evelyn knew that Tom was meeting that crew. But Tom was experienced, and everyone told her that surely Tom was all right. "At 11:30 that night, the phone rang. Oh, how I didn't want to pick up the receiver." The voice on the other end announced that Evelyn was a widow. "There had been a burnover and an entrapment. Four were missing on a hill and then it was confirmed that they were dead. One of them is your husband."

"I dropped to my knees and started screaming. I was in a daze for six months afterward. I just want my husband back and my children want Daddy to come home. He was my best friend in life. I miss him so. I miss him so much."

For Jason Emhoff, his long road to recovery began in the front seat of the van when the Entiat Hot Shots EMTs came to his aid. Mike Pipgras, Derek Birks, and Jody Tate cleaned and bandaged him and prepared him for transportation to a burn unit in Seattle. "I won't ever forget them. Right then I knew it was going to be all right." He sustained first-, second-, and third-degree burns over approximately 40 percent of his body. The small fingers on both his hands were burned off. It has been a long road back for him. The burden was shared with his mother and father, who visited him every day in the hospital. Emhoff has returned to wildlands firefighting. His incredibly positive nature allows him to educate younger firefighters on some of the things he knows about.

Rebecca Welch got burned that day, but not badly—only second-degree. One of the campers said to a forestry service supervisor in a telephone conversation, "There's no question that she saved us. No doubt about it at all. We would have died. Her first reaction was to help us. That says a lot about her and who she is. It was a very human thing to do. She did it without hesitation . . . there are no words to express what she did . . . it was truly a life-or-death situation." She was honored for her remarkable act of bravery with the Department of Agriculture Secretary's Honor Award for Heroism. She too has returned to fighting fires for the forestry service. In addition, she received the Carnegie Hero Fund Commission Medal for risking her life to an extraordinary degree while saving two other persons. She was also awarded Rotary International's Paul Harris Award for Heroism and the Red Cross's Heroism Award. Stihl Corporation gave her its National Forestry Heroism Award. Rebecca is not only the first woman to be honored by Stihl, but the youngest person.

Emily Hinson came very close to being burned that afternoon, but she wasn't. As soon as she could, she called home to inform her mother that she had a close call, but she was all right and not to worry. Hinson remembers hearing over the radio from Ellreese Daniels that they were preparing for a deployment of their shelters just to be safe. "I didn't even begin to grasp the seriousness of the situation. Even when the first word came in that some were missing, it never occurred to me they might be dead. Then Pete Kampen gathered us all together and he was crying and he told us what had happened. We all cried a lot."

At the Hinson household, Jim, Emily's father, arrived home from work that evening. "I sat down to watch the news and there was the Thirty-Mile Fire story. What my wife told me about the close call didn't impact me. I had been a firefighter and I knew that sometimes happened, and I knew Em was all right. When Karen FitzPatrick's picture flashed on the screen—all I saw was my Em's face and I started to cry. Intellectually I understood that Em was OK, but I had to see her and hold her.

"We spent that night in the car, driving to where she was. When I saw her, I ran to her and held her so tight. I told her that I loved her and didn't know what I would do without her in my life."

What started out as a little campfire ended up sweeping away so many dreams. It didn't matter what your relationship was to the forestry service, the Thirty-Mile Fire left a scar on your heart. On the one hand, Rebecca Welch was willing to sacrifice her life to save others. And on the other hand, Karen FitzPatrick, believed to be the youngest career firefighter killed in America by fire, died only one month after her high school graduation.

Tom Craven, Karen FitzPatrick, Jessica Johnson, and Devin Weaver are heroes not because they died fighting a fire, but because they were willing to risk their own safety for that of others and because of their indomitable spirit in life.

17

IMPALED

September 3, 1991

Rolling Hills Estates, California

Tod Mitcham

"Person trapped, 21 Peartree Lane," was the call that sent Los Angeles County Firefighter Specialist Tod Mitcham to a place he had never been before. It wasn't a location; it was a call to summon inner strength and courage deep inside and risk his own life in effecting a type of rescue he had never even seen before—let alone attempted—to try to save the life of twenty-four-year-old construction worker Andres de la Hoya.

Urban Search and Rescue Unit One (USAR-1) was returning from the training center where Mitcham and members of his unit had been training other firefighters in search-and-rescue techniques. En route to the call, which took about twenty minutes, Mitcham and his captain, Reggie Lee, discussed what they might find once they got there. Engine 106, who was first on the scene, met them when they arrived.

"They showed us a forty-five-foot excavation hole that had been drilled to use as a concrete footing for hillside erosion control behind a

163

Tod Mitcham is suspended upside down holding a cutting torch, being lowered into the shaft.

large home being built in the area. It was about thirty-six inches wide, and there was a steel reinforcing cage inside the hole. About twenty-five feet down was Andres, who had lost his balance and fell and was impaled on a piece of one-inch-thick rebar (reinforcement bar). The bar went through his upper left arm and out his shoulder.

"We noticed there was a fair amount of blood loss," Mitcham remembers. "His consciousness level was low because of a combination of blood loss and lack of oxygen. Ventilation fans were put in place and almost immediately the victim's level of consciousness improved."

It was imperative that the victim's condition be assessed before any rescue could be implemented. Los Angeles County Firefighter Specialist/ Paramedic Daniel Harney was lowered feetfirst down to Andres. He read Andres's vital signs and determined that the prognosis looked good for a successful rescue. While Harney was in the hole, Mitcham and Captain Lee discussed the rescue plan.

"Captain Lee and I came up with a plan regarding how to effect the rescue. The victim needed to be stabilized so he couldn't fall deeper into the hole. He could still possibly fall twenty-plus feet deeper, which would only further complicate the rescue. We planned to have three lines down there, one attached to me, one to him, and the third to both of us. Once that was accomplished, I would cut the one-inch-thick bar he was impaled upon.

"Using a cutting torch, I practiced on a piece of rebar so I knew just how long it would take to burn through it. We were concerned about how hot the bar would get and whether or not it would burn Andres when I cut it. Surprisingly, the heat didn't carry very far, which made the process easier, as I wouldn't have to cut the bar so far away from his arm."

As if it weren't dicey enough to go into a small hole, stabilize an impaled victim, burn through the rod that had him trapped, and at the same time save him from falling, none of this could be accomplished in the position Tod Mitcham had trained in—upright. He needed to be lowered into the hole and cut the victim out while hanging upside down.

If he was lowered feetfirst, the sparks and molten steel would fall on him, causing burns.

"We carry an oxygen-acetylene torch on the USAR truck, but our gas lines were too short to reach down into the hole where Andres was trapped. Luckily, the construction crew had long lines on their torch. It looked like everything we could plan for had been considered and it was time to go. I wore a rescue harness that was very suitable for this type of rescue. We trained with these harnesses and had a lot of faith in them.

"Reggie Lee stayed right at the entrance to the hole and kept a steady stream of conversation with me to make sure I was all right. It is always the same in these types of situations: one person does all the sexy stuff and gets the attention, but the many men involved—like Reggie—are the reasons why these rescues are successful. Honestly, I was just one of a crew. I knew with my captain up there watching out for me, I would be fine. He told me that the moment I didn't sound just right, I was out of there. He could have easily taken my place and done the rescue, but it made more sense for me because I was smaller and the space down there was pretty confining.

"Then I was on my way down. When I got down about fifteen feet or so, I started to feel really bad. It felt like the walls were closing in on me. At the same time, I knew Andres was depending on me. I told them to stop me for a minute. There is a technique we train for in just such a situation. I closed my eyes and took four long, slow breaths. With each one of them, I could feel the anxiety ebbing. I told myself that when I opened my eyes, I had to focus on every task I had to accomplish, and I did. Then they continued lowering me until I reached him.

"When I got down to Andres, I had my first chance to really assess the situation. I have to say that my initial thought was, How am I going to do this? It was a good thing Andres couldn't get inside my head.

"He was really studying me and what I was doing. One of the small problems we were faced with was a language barrier. Andres didn't speak much English and my Spanish is pretty sparse. We certainly weren't going to have any in-depth conversations. At one point, I touched the rebar cage and it moved. That was all it took and he spoke much better English, asking me to please not touch the steel cage.

"It was very important to stabilize him so that when I cut the steel bar, he would not move. In effect I had to suspend him, and then cut the rod. It was a funny thing; when I was being lowered down I became worried, but when I got down there and started working to free him, all I thought about was the job at hand. Those four breaths had done their job."

Up top, Captain Lee's voice did not betray his concern for his firefighter. By then, Mitcham had been upside down for almost twenty minutes. Should he lose consciousness and have to be rescued, it could be very difficult to pull him out of the hole if his body became relaxed. The captain's stream of questions and observations was unceasing, as were Mitcham's responses.

Then it was time to make the cut. The gas was turned on and the torch lit on the first attempt. Within ten seconds, the bar was split. The cutting process was over almost as soon as it started. Now it was time to leave.

"Andres was in a lot of pain, and we needed to get him to the top and off to the hospital as soon as possible. I was pleased that he was still so alert after all the time he spent hanging there. If he slipped into shock, it could have all been over."

The process of extricating both men from the hole was tedious. Mitcham was above the victim and would be raised about a foot, and then Andres would be raised the same distance. It was important to keep them together in case something happened to the victim. Several minutes later, Firefighter Mitcham's boots were visible. They kept raising him until Andres was completely out of the hole. They had to get him to the waiting helicopter and on his way to Harbor General Hospital before Mitcham could be taken down.

Andres de la Hoya made a full recovery. Miraculously, the one-inch steel rod that had pierced his arm and come out above his shoulder missed several vital blood vessels. His life could have ended in so many ways, but it did not that day.

Tod Mitcham was part of a small group of firefighters honored as the first recipients of the Los Angeles County Fire Department's Medal of Valor for risking his life with heroic and aggressive actions that saved the life of another.

In reflection, Tod Mitcham was happy to be recognized, but made it clear he was just part of a team and no more. Captain Reggie Lee stated that Mitcham exemplified the very best of the Los Angeles County Fire Department and firefighters everywhere.

18

"I'M ALWAYS EITHER IN THE RIGHT PLACE OR THE WRONG ONE ALL THE TIME"

April 8, 1990

Brookfield, Ohio

David Coffy

Mark Timko had just gone to bed. His wife, Patricia, was still downstairs and the children were sleeping on the second floor. At about one in the morning, Mark was awakened by his wife screaming that a fire was downstairs. He ran down and found the sofa had caught on fire. Patricia had apparently fallen asleep with a lit cigarette in her hand. Together, they turned it over and Mark beat the flames out using a pillow. Thinking that the fire was extinguished, he said they should pull the sofa out through the front door. With her pushing and him pulling, they got the still-smoldering piece of furniture to the doorway. Once there, it burst into flames again, trapping her in the front room and him outside on the porch. He yelled at her to get the children out of the house.

David Coffy, Brookfield, Ohio, Fire Department.

He left the porch, intending to reenter the house through the side door. But first, he found a garden hose and returned to the front door and began putting water on the fire, which had started to engulf the front room. Then, he ran to the side door and opened it. As he entered, the first floor flashed over, sending flames up the staircase. He heard his wife calling for help from the second floor, but he was unable to get to her, as the entire first floor was a sea of flames.

At about the same time, Tom Bayus was driving home and saw the fire. He stopped briefly to assess the situation and continued to the next street where he lived. He told his mother of the fire, and she immediately placed a call to the fire department. It was 1:40 A.M. when the call came in reporting a house fire at 7343 Warren Sharon Road.

Today, the Brookfield, Ohio, Fire Department is mostly a full-time department, but it wasn't that way in 1990. On April 8 of that year, Captain David Coffy was the only firefighter on duty in the station. In those days, the 911 system wasn't in place, which meant that all fire calls came in directly to the fire station.

"As soon as the call came in, I set off all the pagers to summon the volunteers to the location of the fire. I was at the fire three minutes later. As I pulled up to the house on Warren Sharon Road in Engine 1, I could see a large volume of fire coming from the front of the residence. I tried to pull into the driveway, but someone had blocked it with his car. I had to stop momentarily for it to be moved. I broadcast a quick report to the responding volunteers that we had a working fire at the location.

"The house was a two-and-a-half-story structure, and when it flashed over, every window was blown out. At that time, all the fire was concentrated on the first floor. I parked the truck, got out, and pulled on the rest of my turnout gear, helmet, and Nomex hood and slipped on my SCBA. Several bystanders approached me and told me that children were trapped on the second floor. They told me the bedroom was located at the rear." He also learned another bedroom was off the rear bedroom, which was where the three-year-old twin boys, Luke and Daniel Timko, were likely trapped. An older boy had luckily gone to stay at a friend's house that night.

"At that time, Brookfield Township Police Chief Tom Jones and Officer Peter Pizzulo approached me and asked what they could do to help. I asked them to remove a twenty-four-foot ladder from the engine and place it at the rear of the house against the second-floor bedroom window."

As soon as the ladder was in place, Officer Pizzulo, who had prior fire experience as a lieutenant on a volunteer fire department, went up and checked the bedroom. Realizing that he had no way to enter the smoke-filled room without protective equipment, he went back down. Then Captain Coffy ascended the ladder and broke out the window. The smoke conditions were very heavy inside the house, and Officer Pizzulo went back up the ladder behind the captain to back him up. The captain asked him to retrieve an inch-and-a-half line from the engine and bring it back to him. Coffy radioed to the volunteers that children were trapped inside. He then climbed in through the window and fell to the floor.

"It was very hot inside the room. I knew that even with my protective gear, it was going to be tough. The smoke was banked all the way to the floor. It was a heavy, black smoke, the kind that supports a flashover. I needed the hose to lower the temperature in the room. If it flashed, it wasn't likely that anyone was coming out of the room, including me."

Within a minute or two, Pizzulo returned with the hose. He had not charged the line, leaving that job for the engineer who was only a minute away from arriving. As he stood on the ladder, a blast of hot air hit him, and within seconds, Officer Pizzulo received first-degree burns to his face and his uniform was singed. But he stood his ground. "Children were trapped up there and a firefighter was risking his own life searching for them. I wasn't going anywhere."

Captain Coffy started to look for the children. "I did a right-hand search pattern. As I moved through the room, I could feel several items on the floor that were melting from the heat. Later, I found out they were plastic toys. While I searched, the officer remained in place at the top of the ladder.

"As I searched that room, I found a door that led to another room so I closed it. I had been told that this was the children's room and by shutting the door, I could keep some of the heat away from that room. If I came up dry in the first room, I would simply open the door and continue my search.

"Although it was nighttime, it meant nothing because it wasn't possible to see anything anyway. I continued along the wall, and I came to something. Using my gloved hands, I began feeling it and determined it was a crib. All this time I had been crawling on the floor, trying to stay as low as I could to keep away from the heat as much as possible. I raised myself up and reached over the top of the crib and felt around with my gloved hands. There he was—an unconscious child. I picked him up, turned around, and started to go back to the window I had come in. In a matter of a minute, I was lost. At one point I crawled headfirst into a wall."

At that time, the captain began calling to Officer Pizzulo. Over and over he called out, and each time the officer called back, guiding the firefighter to the window. Even with his protective gear, the heat was so intense that Captain Coffy was already burned, but he was at least able to breathe clean air through his SCBA. The lifeless child had no protection other than the firefighter shielding him from the heat as best he could. He made it to the window and handed the child out to the officer, who in turn went down the ladder to a waiting rescue truck. Still upstairs in the room, Coffy was in trouble.

"The heat was too intense for me to stay. I knew my neck was burned and the heat was continuing to rise. I had originally broken out only the bottom pane of the double-hung window when I entered. That forced all the heat out of that same window.

"I went out of the window headfirst. When I did, my SCBA got hung up on the window frame. I finally freed myself and stood on the ladder. I discovered that the hose Officer Pizzulo had brought up had been charged. Then, I broke out the upper window and the wooden frame that divided the window in half. Removing the upper window really helped to ventilate the room.

"I was sure the room was ready to flash over at any moment, so I took the hose and sprayed the ceiling of the room for about ten seconds. Then I went back inside the house.

"I began searching in the same room where I had found the first child. Before I had done a right-hand search; this time I went to the left. Right away I ran into the second crib. Just as in the first one, a lifeless child was inside. He was like a rag doll hanging limply in my arms. I shielded him from the heat as best I could and made my way back to the ladder.

"The officer had returned to the top of the ladder, and I handed him the little boy. I watched as he went down the ladder. When he got to the bottom, he ran around to the paramedic unit. Then I prepared to leave the house. Just as I climbed out onto the ladder, Officer Pizzulo came around to the back of the house again. Another person was missing. The children's mother was unaccounted for and thought to be on the second floor."

In the front of the burning house, paramedics worked feverishly to save the lives of the little boys as their father looked on. They were both in respiratory arrest. By now, Captain Coffy had suffered second-degree burns, and yet he climbed back inside the house for a third rescue attempt.

"We didn't know where the mother was located. I could hear the fire burning below me by then, and when I got near the top of the stairs, I could see the fire coming onto the second floor. I pulled the charged hose line with me when I reentered, and I intended to use it to keep the fire off me if necessary. With fire making its way up to the second level, the chance for a flashover was increasing again.

"I pulled the hose as far as it would stretch and left it. The smoke was still banked down to the floor, and visibility remained at near zero. I went back through the children's room and entered into another hallway. I just kept going to the right and found another bedroom. I could still hear the fire burning and things breaking. I tried not to think about that and just concentrated on my search.

"The next bedroom was empty. This was the older boy's, but it was empty. At this time I didn't really know where I was, but I had always gone to the right since I came back in the house, so I figured going to the left would lead me out again. I also knew that Officer Pizzulo was taking care of me on the ladder. If all else failed, I would just call for him to guide me back to the window. I headed back out into the hallway, still crawling, and found what I thought was another doorway and went through it.

"There was no floor as I hurried through. I began falling and tumbling downward. Then I came to a stop, and fire was everywhere. I had gone down the stairway and ended up on a landing between the first and second floors. As fast as I could, I went back up the stairs.

"When I got to the top, I made a left turn and went down the hallway to an area I hadn't been before. I found another doorway and entered into another bedroom. I was now in the front of the house. On the floor I found an unconscious woman. It was the twins' mother, Patricia."

Captain Mark Christy was off duty that day, but heard his pager and immediately responded to the fire. While on his way to the fire, he had been in radio communication with Captain Coffy and knew he was on the second floor involved in search-and-rescue operations. Even though his first instinct was to join the other captain, he was concerned about the possibility of the fire consuming the entire dwelling and taking everybody's life who was in there.

Christy was the second firefighter to arrive and quickly pulled on his turnout gear and then his SCBA. As he was doing this, he could see that the fire was growing very rapidly.

Christy was set to go in and join Coffy in the search. "The fire was growing so quickly. Just then firefighter Clifford Elliott arrived. I told him to pack up [put on his SCBA] and go inside and help Captain Coffy on the second floor. I grabbed an inch-and-a-half preconnect line and began putting water on the fire. I stayed with it and actually was able to knock most of the fire down in a fairly short amount of time."

By electing to not enter the structure and put water on the fire Captain Christy very probably prevented a flashover from occurring and saved the lives of two firefighters. On the second floor, Captain Coffy noticed a change in the conditions on the second floor as the temperature began to fall. He prepared to pull the woman out into the hallway.

"She was lying face up with her head pointed toward the doorway. Her arms were underneath her body. I started to pull her along the floor, back to the window where the ladder and Officer Pizzulo were. In the hallway I was met by volunteer firefighter Cliff Elliott."

As rapidly as they could, Coffy and Elliott made their way to the back bedroom and passed the unconscious woman to Officer Pizzulo on the ladder.

As he carried her down the ladder, Pizzulo reflected that it was amazing what a person could do with a little adrenaline in his system. When he got her down, Officer Pizzulo ran around to the front of the house and put her down on the roadway. She had third-degree burns over much of her body and was not breathing, so he administered CPR to her in an attempt to save her life.

Captain David Coffy was transported to the hospital that night to have his burns treated. He knew he had given it his best effort but he felt certain that the children were gone. He wasn't sure about the mother. It was hard to tell because everything was so dark in there. In the emergency room he was waiting to be seen by a doctor. It was very noisy, and he asked one of the nurses what the commotion was. It was then he learned that both of the children were alive.

They both had second- and third-degree burns over much of their bodies. One of them had the fingers on one hand burned off. But they were still alive.

"I asked if it was all right if saw I them. I just wanted to look at them and see they were alive. When I looked at them, it felt so good to know they weren't dead." That night they were both transported to the Akron Burn Center, where they recovered.

Sadly, the paramedics were unable to resuscitate their mother, and she died. She was badly burned over most of her body and had inhaled a large amount of superheated toxic gases.

Captain David Coffy was named Ohio State Firefighter of the Year. He also received the number two Firefighter of the Year award from *Firehouse* magazine as part of their Heroism and Community Service program. Additionally, Coffy received an award from the United States Congress for his heroic rescue.

Officer Peter Pizzulo and Firefighter Clifford Elliott received awards for their heroism in aiding Captain Coffy. Without Officer Pizzulo's vigilance at the window, it isn't possible to predict what might have happened when Captain Coffy became disoriented while trying to bring one of the twins to safety. In addition, Pizzulo carried all three of the victims down the ladder. He also gave the captain moral support that made it possible for him to continue the rescue of the second child and the final victim. Firefighter Elliott was the second man inside the house. Had Captain Coffy encountered difficulty, Elliott would have had to rescue him. At a time when the heat and a long period of exertion had taken its toll on the firefighter, Elliott was there for him. In addition, they had no assurance that a total flashover of the second floor wouldn't take place.

This was the third of many incredible rescues Captain David Coffy has undertaken. "It just seems like I'm always either in the right place or the wrong one all the time. It has gone that way my whole career, since that night on Warren Sharon Road."

Captain Coffy has also been inducted into the Ohio State Firefighters Hall of Fame. Not too bad for a man who as a little boy used to hang around the fire station and help wash the trucks.

19

A CHRISTMAS EVE PARTY

December 24, 2000

Chicago, Illinois

Wayne Gayda

The week before Christmas of 2000, the city of Chicago had a large snowstorm. By the time Christmas Eve arrived, the streets were a mess. Ice, slush, and piles of snow made it difficult for passenger cars to maneuver, let alone fire trucks. That night, Chicago Fire Department's Lieutenant Wayne Gayda was assigned to Truck 32. At 7:26 P.M., they received a call to 2002 South Spaulding Avenue for a heavy fire at a three-story apartment.

As the truck approached the fire, crowds of people lined the street. Cars were parked everywhere, and the engine couldn't access the fire hydrant on the corner nearest the fire.

"By the time we got the aerial apparatus truck into position in front of the building, flames were blowing out of the windows from the basement and first floor," Gayda remembers. "The basement actually came

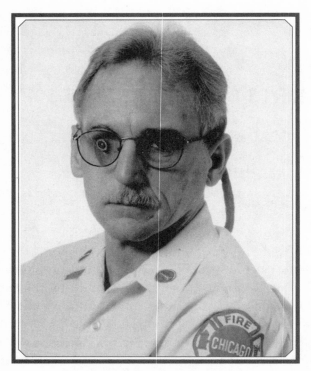

Wayne Gayda, Chicago Fire Department.

up to about one half of a regular story instead of being flush with the ground. We were told that many people were trapped on the third floor.

"There was no way to make an entrance in the front; the fire was too intense. Our aerial ladder was useless with the way the fire was coming out of the windows. A firefighter trying to enter the apartment off the end of the ladder would have been climbing into a cauldron of fire. I left some of the men to try and position the ladder with the thought that we might be able to use it as we knocked down the fire. Then, I ran around to the back of the building and went in that way. I had on my turnout gear, Nomex hood, gloves, helmet, and my SCBA. I went up an enclosed staircase to the second floor. All of the fire was in the basement and the first floor, but it was lapping up to the second floor.

"Up on the second floor, I couldn't really see anything because of the smoke; it was like walking into the night. The smoke was banked down all the way to the floor. When I went to the door, I had to use my ax to break it open, and then I crawled in.

"I didn't know the floor layout of the house, and I was concerned about not becoming lost in there. I was alone, and because we were short on manpower that night, I didn't think there would be anybody backing me up right away. I tried to keep my bearings as I went from room to room, searching on my hands and knees.

"I started off in the kitchen, and after I cleared that room, I moved out into what was probably a hallway. Then I went into a bathroom. So far, I had found nothing; the floor seemed deserted. Next was a bedroom and again nothing. After that, I went into the living room. A television had been left on, which gave off some light in the smoke-filled room. As I moved forward, I was spreading out my hands to feel for something.

"I was a long way from the kitchen by now, and I was keeping the path back to the stairwell in my mind. Then I felt something. It was an unconscious woman on the floor. I didn't know it then, but I had found a seventy-seven-year-old lady.

"Because of the heat in the room, I couldn't stand up, so I stayed in my crawl position and began to pull her back to the exit. The flames were coming up from the first floor and lapping into the room we were in. I didn't even take the time to see if she was breathing; the only concern I had was getting her out. When I got her to the stairway landing, I was met by one of my firefighters. I gave her to him and went back in again.

"I knew I had checked most of the rooms on that floor, but I wanted to make sure I didn't miss anyone. I found my way back to the living room and completed my search. Then I began to feel along the walls, looking for a door. I found one that I thought probably led to another bedroom. I tried to open it, but it was jammed.

"Once again, I used my ax. A tremendous amount of heat and smoke was inside this room, and there was plenty of fire. The windows were broken out, and the fire on the first floor was coming in through them. I began to search, and I found one person, then another, then another, and finally one more. All of them were unconscious, and I was certain they were burned as well. I didn't know how many people there were in all, but I knew I had found several, including an infant.

"I found the baby first—a twenty-eight-day-old little girl. She was so small she could fit in my hand. I took my SCBA mask off and put it over her face. The mask itself was almost as big as she was. Then I crawled as fast as I could to the stairway. The conditions were so bad that I knew I had no time to spare. I passed her off to a paramedic. I put my mask back on and went in again.

"The next person I grabbed was the mother. She was on the floor like the others. When I went back into the room, it was cooler. The windowsills and curtains were still on fire, but the firefighters down on the street were obviously putting water on the blaze, which was lowering the temperature.

"I pulled the mother along the floor back to the staircase and gave her to Lieutenant Bob Molinari. By the time I got her out, I was starting to run out of strength. But there were still two more children in the room. I didn't know it then, but none of the three people I had already brought out was breathing.

"All I was thinking about was getting the people out. When I started back in for the fourth victim, I ran out of air; there was so much noise from the fire I hadn't heard my low-air alarm. When that happens, the facepiece sucks against your face. There isn't any override that lets the outside air in; you go to nothing, just as though you put your hand over your mouth. When that happened, I pulled my facepiece off and kept going; I couldn't turn around. I didn't know how many people were in there. What would have happened if I went back for another bottle?

"I am not saying it's right, but I'm from the old school. If I have to breathe smoke and bad air, that's the way it goes. Maybe it's a curse, but I can deal with the smoke, and I find that using the facepiece dulls my senses.

"I had lost my right eye to cancer, and after I got better, I worked really hard to come back to the job. I had to take a lot of tests to prove I could still do it. I felt I had more to do as a firefighter. Since the loss of one of my eyes, when I don't use my facepiece I see and feel better. That isn't to say I won't use it when things get really bad, but if given a preference and choice, I would rather go without it.

"The next person I brought out was a little girl. She was about eleven years old. By then, the fire had been knocked down in the front of the building. Firefighters were able to make their way up to the second floor. They knew from the people being brought down that a lot of victims were on that floor.

"Firefighter Caesar Cabral made his way up to the window on a ladder. He climbed into the window where I found the others. He was able to rescue the last victim, the sister of the little girl I had just taken out. She was ten years old."

What Lieutenant Gayda didn't know was that another battle was going on in the front of the building. The paramedics and firefighters were fighting to save the lives of the five victims. When they were brought out, they were lifeless. In a desperate move, one of the paramedics performed an emergency tracheotomy on one of the little girls. All of them were burned from the hot gases and flames. While this was going on, the lieutenant went back in again. The search was not over yet.

"I had no idea how many people we were going to find, and all we knew was that we had taken five people out of there so far. We continued our search until the floor was clear. As it turned out, there were no more people to rescue. The youngest person that came out of there was less than a month old and the oldest was seventy-seven. By the end, I hit the wall. I was exhausted. After the fire was out, it was back to the station to clean up and get ready for the next one."

As it turned out, no firefighters were injured at 2002 South Spaulding that night. The battle in front of the house and later in the hospital was also won. Everyone not only lived but also made a complete recovery. They didn't have Christmas that year, but they had their lives. Some months later, the baby's mother said she thinks of firefighters every day when she looks into the eyes of her baby. Then she begins to cry as she hugs her little one close.

The firefighters of the companies who fought the fires and saved the victims' lives were not done yet. They all contributed to make sure Christmas came the following year. A battalion chief found out that one of the little girls had always wanted to play the trombone, so he bought her one. The firefighters of Truck 32 feel the family is part of the firehouse family now and always will be.

For his nearly unparalleled heroism in the face of death, Wayne Gayda was awarded a Medal of Valor from the city of Chicago. He won the Firefighter of the Year award from *Firehouse* magazine for his heroic actions that night.

On a later Christmas, another fire caused Gayda to cross paths with danger. He and his wife were out shopping and he saw smoke. "I thought I better check it out. I went in and found a fire on the first floor of a three-story apartment building. The stairwell doors were left open, and the fire was blowing all the way to the top floor. I started searching for people. I found an eighty-year-old lady and got her down. I was told that a man was trapped on the third floor. The fire was getting bad, and I didn't have any protective gear. My wife was very frightened, but I told her that I had to go back in. I made my way up there to where he was. He was hanging out of a window, and the first fire unit that arrived put a ladder up just in time and got him before he fell." For that rescue, he was awarded a second Medal for Valor from the City of Chicago.

Not all of the rescues have gone so well. While trying to rescue a three-year-old girl, Lieutenant Gayda ended up trapped in the fire. After finding her, he couldn't get out. He finally found a window, broke it, and left with the little girl. "I won't ever forget that little girl. Her name was Crystal and she fought hard to make it, but it didn't happen and she died. I won't ever forget her."

When asked about the rescue that Christmas Eve in 2000, Lieutenant Wayne Gayda said, "A lot of people were doing things that night. I was just one person. Everybody there received a unit commendation. You know, if you took any one of us out of the mix that night, it wouldn't have come out the way it did." Reflecting back on the awards he has received he said, "There are a lot of people who are heroes and nobody notices. That night I just got the spotlight, that's all."

Wayne was right about coming back to firefighting after losing his eye. He did have more to do.

20

"SHE MIGHT AS WELL HAVE BEEN MILES AWAY"

August 27, 1999

Hudson Falls, New York

Paul Martin

Hudson Falls, New York, an old mill town nestled on the Hudson River, has had a volunteer fire department since 1880. Just before 1 A.M. on August 27, 1999, a call came in to the dispatch center for a structure fire at 56 John Street. Assistant Chief Paul Martin received the call over his radio and was en route from his home.

"I got there just a couple of minutes after the engine company. I did a quick assessment of the fire situation. Chief Paul Dietrich arrived right after I did, and we discussed some strategy. The configuration of the house was in a sort of cross and split up into several little apartments, but the fire had a pretty good hold on the first floor.

"Flames were blowing out of the porch on the street side. I was look-ing at it as I pulled on my gear. I had my full turnouts, helmet, and SCBA.

Paul Martin, Hudson Falls, New York, Fire Department.

People were screaming that a woman was trapped in the front room. Firefighter Steven Smith was on the front porch trying to force the door. A tremendous amount of heat was in that area. Finally, the heat was too much, and it drove him away from the door. He pushed hard on it but could only get it open partway. After he left, I hit the door with everything I had. With each hit of my shoulder, the door opened a bit more until there was enough room for me to get through.

"When I got it open, flames were pouring out of the top portion. Flames shot like a blowtorch from a window that was just to my side, and they were rolling underneath the roof of the porch. I could see inside the front room. The smoke conditions weren't too bad, but nearly everything in the room was on fire.

"Lying down on my stomach on the floor, I started into the room. I could see the woman. She was lying on the floor in the middle of the room. In a normal situation, it wouldn't take more than three or four seconds to walk over to her, but not now. With all the fire in the room, she might as well have been miles away. I figured she was already critically burned. I knew the chances of me getting burned were good, and I had no idea whether she was alive or not. But it didn't matter; I was going to go after her.

"I was already feeling tremendous heat. I was sort of having a two-sided conversation with myself as I started in. 'Wow, this is hot.' 'I know it's hot, but you can't stop.' I knew I had to keep going. She was about fifteen to twenty feet away from me, and everything was on fire around us. I felt like I was about the only thing not on fire in that room.

"It was hard to say if the room had flashed over because the floor wasn't burning, but the walls were burning almost all the way to the floor. All of the furniture was in flames as well. I could see into the kitchen, and the table was totally engulfed. It seemed odd to me that even the books in the bookcases were burning. I'd never seen that before. Usually the bookcases burn leaving the books more or less intact, but with the enormous amount of heat everything was going.

"Deeper inside, I could see why we had so much trouble getting in. A heavy bed frame was partially blocking the door. The residents were no longer using that door, and it had been barred and locked. I pushed the heavy metal frame away and got the door all the way open.

"I snaked my way across the floor to the woman. By the time I reached her, I could tell I was starting to burn from the feeling on my ears. I have been burned before in my career, and I just wrote it off at that point. It's part of the job."

Outside on the porch, other firefighters waited at the door. Some of them did not have SCBAs, but they were watching to make sure Chief Martin was all right. It was likely that if things didn't go well, they couldn't do much to help.

"When I got to the woman, I was still on my stomach. I raised myself up in an attempt to get a good grip on her, but the heat was too much. I couldn't even get to a crouched position. It was incredibly hot on the floor, but even a foot higher was unbearable. The only way I could even think of surviving in that environment was by staying on the floor.

"To extract her, I would have to stay down and pull her along the floor. I knew it was hot, but I didn't know I was being damaged. My back, legs, and hips were being subjected to a lot of heat, and I was feeling pain, but I couldn't stop.

"I had to go on, for myself. I had her in my arms and I couldn't let her go. The only way she wouldn't get out with me was if I didn't get out.

"I was making progress and I was able to get her to the doorway, but I was running out of steam. The heat had sapped my strength. I wasn't going to be able to pull her any farther without raising up into a crouching position no matter how hot it was.

"Every conscious thought I had in that room was in some way connected to getting her out of there. When I saw the fire, I thought she had to come out right away. The heat just gave me the same thought. The burns I felt brought the same response. And now I knew I had to move into the hot zone, actually the even hotter zone, since it was all hot.

"I moved up to a crouch and I was right, it was bad up there. I put my arms around her and braced my boot against the door and pushed with everything I had and actually got her three-quarters of the way through. Then Firefighters Bob Buser and Roger Corlew, who were from the neighboring town fire department of Kingsbury, came to my aid. They both pulled on her arms. That was all we needed and she was out. I doubt that I would have been capable of getting her out on my own.

"I knew I had to get away from the heat, I couldn't take it anymore. I rolled away from the door and tumbled off onto the ground. Immediately I tore my mask off and slipped out of my SCBA. I took my turnout coat off and I thought, Now I'll be able to cool off. But that didn't happen. I was still burning up. After about twenty seconds, I was still feeling no relief and I pulled my suspenders off and dropped my turnout pants.

"When I left my house, I had on a T-shirt and sweatpants over cotton gym shorts. By then Chief Dietrich came over to me and confirmed that no one else was in the house. My hip was really hurting then and I reached down to rub it. When I looked down, I could see that large parts of my sweatpants and shirt were just gone.

"I rubbed the spot and my skin made a 'ssshhhh' sound. It all just popped and came off in my hands. It still didn't quite click with me as to what had happened. The feeling of heat still hadn't gone away, and I walked over to the EMS unit and said, 'I think I got a little burned back here or something.' The paramedic looked at me and said, 'You've got more than a little bit. Get in here and lie down.' With that, I was on my way to the hospital.

"When I got to the emergency room, I was pretty uncomfortable. I wasn't that concerned about me; I wanted to know how the lady was doing. I kept asking, and they finally told me that they had called for a medivac helicopter to transport her to a burn treatment center in Westchester County, just outside of New York City. That was when I knew how serious her injuries really were. Then someone handed me a phone and said it was my wife.

"What's going on? Are you OK?"

"Yeah. I got a little burned, it's no big deal."

Chief Martin lay on his stomach in the emergency room talking to his wife while a team of nurses and doctors worked on his burns. He didn't know it, but he had a large area of third-degree and significant second-degree burns on his body. He was seriously injured but was taking it all in stride.

He was subjected to temperatures of more than a thousand degrees inside the burning room. Being so involved in the rescue, he didn't realize that his protective clothing had been defeated by the high temperatures. Turnout coats and pants are fireproof under the very high temperatures firefighters normally face on a daily basis. Paul Martin's were charred and actually burned through in some places. This gear is made in three layers: the outer fire retardant shell; the next layer, a vapor barrier that allows perspiration to escape but prevents moisture, such as water or steam, from passing through; and the final layer, which is a quilted thermal layer. The vapor barrier actually ignited on his gear, which, in turn, destroyed the thermal layer; and his T-shirt and sweatpants caught on fire next to his skin. Had he not removed his turnouts as soon as he was clear of the house, the fire would have continued to burn him.

"About fifteen minutes after I finished talking with my wife, I looked up and there she was, standing in the emergency room with me. It had been her worst nightmare since the time when we were first dating—that something would happen to me. And now she was facing it.

"She walked in and took my hand. I could see the concern on her face, but she held it in while they were working on me. She was a real trooper."

Looking at her husband, she remembered the time after they first met. "When Paul and I first started dating, a Hudson Falls firefighter named Paul MacMurray was killed in a fire and that was always in the back of my mind. Even though the nurses told me his burns were not life-threatening, standing there looking down at him lying on the gurney was one of the scariest moments in my life. I thought about what could have happened and what could possibly happen in the future."

The treatment Martin received in the emergency room was the beginning of a long series of painful procedures he would undergo. Daily, grueling treatments stripped away the dead tissue. Then came surgical skin grafts to repair the damage done by the fire.

The elderly woman he rescued remained in the burn unit for about thirty days before she succumbed to her injuries. She never regained consciousness and remained on a respirator until her death.

It wasn't until December 1999 that the chief returned to his duties at the fire department. An investigation into the cause of the fire traced its origin to a faulty clothes dryer in the rear of the house.

Assistant Chief Paul Martin received the first Medal of Valor from the Hudson Falls Volunteer Fire Department. He was *Firehouse* magazine's grand prize recipient for Community Service and Valor. Additionally, he was the Hudson Valley Fireman's Association Firefighter of the Year. In the United States Congress, a proclamation detailing his extraordinary heroic actions was read into the Congressional Record.

For his actions, Hudson Falls Volunteer Fire Department Firefighter Steven Smith received a *Firehouse* magazine Legion of Merit Award for his brave actions at the front door that night, remaining there and attempting to open the door to gain access to the residence. He continued his duties until he was driven off the porch by the flames and heat that burned his turnout gear.

To this day, Paul Martin continues as the assistant chief of his department. "It was good to get back my duties." He is also a deputy bureau chief with the New York State Fire Marshal's Office.

21

THE SILHOUETTE

June 5, 1988

Columbus, Ohio

Samuel Towns

When the phone rings in the middle of the night, it rarely brings good news. It is the same at any firehouse. On June 5, 1988, Samuel Towns was working at the Columbus, Ohio, Fire Department's Ladder Company 8, and a little after two in the morning, a call came in to his station house. It wasn't good news. They had a house fire in the 400 block of North Monroe Avenue, and a child was trapped inside.

"We were dispatched along with our engine company. I was the tiller-man on the ladder truck. As we pulled up, I looked at the upper window of the two-story wooden frame house. I thought I saw the silhouette of a child in one of the windows.

"As the truck came to a stop, a woman ran across the front yard screaming, 'My baby's in there!' She said that over and over. I already had all of my equipment on, including an SCBA, as I got off the truck.

Samuel Towns, Columbus, Ohio, Fire Department.

Normally, the two drivers of the ladder truck do outside work at a fire, but I had seen the child up there.

"I grabbed a ladder and put it up to the porch roof. The window that I had seen the child in was directly above the porch. Flames were coming out of every window and door on the ground floor. At the front door, a lot of fire was coming out, and it was rolling along the ceiling of the porch and lapping over the edge of the roof.

"I climbed up on the porch and broke out the window using a short pike pole. This helped to vent the heat out of the room as well as give me a place to go in. I knew that there was a very narrow window of opportunity in which we would have a chance to rescue this child, and I had to seize it.

"I didn't know it at the time, but the incident commander was trying to get my attention, telling me not to go in because they were going to start extinguishing the fire and didn't want to steam me while I was on the second floor. Of course, he didn't realize what I had seen.

"As soon as I broke the window, heavy, black smoke began to pour out. Then in I went and immediately started to do a right-hand search on my hands and knees. I had no intention of remaining in there very long. It was extremely hot in the room, and I could feel heat radiating through the floor and my turnout gear.

"Once before, on a different rescue, I was in a room that flashed over and the conditions inside this room were remarkably similar. I was screaming out to the child, 'Hey! Where are you? Where are you?' Then I listened.

"I could hear the fire crackling downstairs. Actually, it was in the ceiling of the first floor, which was only inches away from me. Then I heard a moaning sound. I stopped again and listened. Again I heard the moaning sound.

"The black smoke was banked all the way down to the floor. All of my searching was being done completely blind. I could hear firefighters outside and the sirens of emergency vehicles still arriving in front of the house. And the moaning."

Because of the rapidity in which Samuel Towns was able to gain entrance to the upstairs floor, he did not have the protection of a hose line. There simply had not been time to pull a preconnect line off an engine. When a firefighter has hose protection, he gains three key advantages. First, the fire can be kept off the firefighter. Second, the room's temperature can be lowered, diminishing the likelihood of a flashover or similar deadly high-heat event. And third, the line can lead back to the place where entrance was made. Firefighter Towns had none of these protections.

"I found a bed in the room and checked it, but no one was in it. Then, I checked all around the bed and again no one. I went past a door leading out of the room, but I continued to check the perimeter. I found another door, opened it, and went in. I thought it might be a closet and it was. Inside was an unconscious nine-year-old boy.

"I tried to pick him up, but each time I did, his skin pulled off in my hands. I couldn't see the child, but I knew he was very badly burned. His skin was literally melting, causing him to slide out of my hands. Finally, I was able to hold him tight to me and I crawled back to the window.

"When I got there, I found that the aerial ladder was up to the window. It was very hard to pass him to the firefighter outside because of his burns. His skin continued to come off and was sticking to my turnout gear. After careful maneuvering, I was able to successfully hand him over.

"I wasn't sure if there were any others on the second floor. I knew if that were the case, they were in serious trouble. I listened, and I could hear noise that could have been more moaning. I thought I should make one more check of the room. I moved over near the door leading out of the room, and I realized the sounds I had heard were firefighters downstairs. I turned back toward the window and it happened. The room flashed over."

Generally speaking, a flashover will increase the temperature in a given space to between 1,000 to 1,500 degrees almost instantly. A firefighter who is completely outfitted with protective clothing has only a couple of seconds to get out before severe burns or death will occur. At the time of the fire, Samuel Towns was in the process of field-testing new turnout gear. These turnouts had superior insulation quality and were supposed to offer a greater measure of protection from heat. He was now going to find out.

"All I could see was red all around me and heat. The room had been hot before, but not like it was then. I was near the window, and I went for the opening as fast as I could. The firefighters who saw it happen said that the flames shot around me and out of the window. I came through the window next.

"My turnout gear worked very well. The fire had burned the back of the coat, but not my body. That is the gear we all now wear in Columbus. I am sure that night was a factor, at least I hope so."

As soon as Towns was clear of the flashover, he returned to his outside duties. "I actually didn't know my gear had even been burned, until later. We had a fire to fight, and I took my place on the team."

When the little boy was brought down the ladder, he had stopped breathing. The paramedics were able to revive him, and off to the hospital they went. He was gravely injured with third-degree burns on more than 90 percent of his body. In the burn center at Columbus Children's Hospital, he was able to hang on for a couple of days, but he ultimately died.

For his extraordinary rescue under the most dangerous of conditions, Firefighter Samuel Towns received many awards, including the number two award from *Firehouse* magazine as part of their Heroism and Community Service program. He also was awarded Medals of Valor from the city of Columbus and the state of Ohio. Numerous business and civic organizations named him their Firefighter of the Year.

"After that night, the little boy's mother thanked me so many times for going and getting him. She kept in contact with me for several years. She said to me, 'You're a real hero, I can't believe you were able to do that.' I never thought of myself that way. I know any other firefighter at the fire that night would have done the same thing.

"In looking back, I would say that I felt the boy's death the most and I didn't like that. I know it wasn't anything that I did or didn't do that caused his death, but just the same, he died. It hurt then and still does. In firefighting, it's like that sometimes and it can't be changed."

22

"THEY ARE CALLING ME A HERO, BUT I DON'T SEE IT"

May 14, 1991

New York, New York

Patrick Barr and Kevin Shea

On May 14, 1991, at 10:58 A.M., Alarm Box 33-837 was transmitted to the New York City Fire Department for a fire at 737 Seventh Avenue in Manhattan. The stage was set for one of the most famous rescues in American firefighting history. Even a picture of the event was judged to be in the top one hundred twentieth-century *New York Post* news photographs. The video of the rescue, known as "The Seventh Avenue Rope Rescue," was nightly news fare from coast to coast and has been included in training films for firefighters around the country.

Patrick "Paddy" Barr was normally assigned to Ladder Company 45, but he had been detailed to Rescue 1 that day because of a manpower shortage. The members of Rescue 1 had returned from a call and were in the firehouse kitchen repacking one of their rescue ropes. The kitchen

Left to right: Patrick Barr, Patrick Brown, and Kevin Shea of the New York City
Fire Department pose with the rope used in their heroic rescue.
Patrick Brown was killed on September 11, 2001.

floor was desirable because it is free from oils or solvents that could weaken the rope. Each rescue unit carries two of these ropes, and after being used on a rescue, each is carefully inspected and returned to its carrying bag. It is extremely important to properly pack the rope in its container so it will play (feed) out without tangling when pulled or when the end of the rope is held and the bag is thrown. It was the first time Barr had ever met some of the firefighters at Rescue 1, including Kevin Shea. Barr and Shea were packing the rope when a call came in and they left the rope on the floor to respond.

Rescue 1 rolled out of the station with only one of its ropes. Before they arrived at the scene, they were dispatched to another call that came in for a working fire on Seventh Avenue. When they originally left the station, they were simply responding to a fire call that had nothing to do with a high-rise rescue. Had they known where they were eventually to be sent, Barr and Shea would have grabbed the rope, packed or not.

As Rescue 1 traveled down Seventh Avenue, Shea looked up at the fire on the twelfth floor. "Smoke was pouring out of the windows on the top floor, but I could see something at one of the windows. Then I realized it wasn't a something—it was a someone. It looked to me like he was in trouble. He appeared to have been driven onto the ledge, probably by the fire, smoke, heat, or maybe all of those."

Shea remembers he was teamed up with another firefighter, Kevin Dowdell, who was on loan that day from another rescue company. "The two of us were assigned as an inside team that day, which meant we went to where the fire was burning. We carried an ax and Halligan tool. [Invented by New York firefighter Huey Halligan, the tool is approximately forty inches long and is a pry bar on one end and ventilation tool on the other. It can punch through plaster, glass, and wood.] The fire was twelve flights up, so we didn't take the elevator because of the risk of being trapped if the electricity cut off.

"We got up to the twelfth floor and found the door. It was locked, so we had to force it. Since this was a commercial building, the doors were very sturdy and opened outward. We tried prying the door open with the Halligan tool, and that didn't work. Then Kevin Dowdell used the ax on the door. After he chopped on it for a bit, I was able to pry it the rest of the way. Once we were able to open the door, we found the room was filled with smoke and fire. There wasn't any way we could enter. The smoke was banked down all the way to the floor. Once the engine company came with hoses, they could hook up to the standpipe and attack the fire, but there was no way to enter without the protection of a hose line.

"Right after we got the door open, Lieutenant Patrick Brown, or Paddy as we all called him, put out a call, 'Rescue 1, urgent, need manpower on the roof!' Kevin Dowdell said he was going to stay and see if he could find a way through the smoke and fire and grab the guy while I went up to help out. It was a very quick walk up, as we were one floor from the roof."

Patrick Barr grabbed the rope bag and a six-foot pole with a steel hook on the end. He was ordered by Lieutenant Brown to go directly to the roof along with Shea.

"By the time I got up there, it was already a desperate situation," Shea remembers. "The guy we had seen before, José Gallegos, was threatening to jump rather than being burned to death.

"There was a building under construction at the same level we were at. A lot of construction workers were yelling across to us that there were people trapped just below us. Lieutenant Brown went over to the parapet and leaned over. He could see José on the ledge below us."

The brick building was probably built between 1880 and 1910. The parapet wall was about three feet high and about two and a half feet thick. Its edge stuck out about a foot from the face of the building.

"I started tying the rope into a harness on myself and Firefighter Patrick O'Keefe was helping me," Barr recalls. "Together we tied the rope into a rescue harness. I figured I was going over the side. Meanwhile, Lieutenant Brown talked to José, trying to calm him down.

"I don't know what Gallegos said to Paddy Brown, but I knew the guy was desperate and going to jump. I was all set to go, but there was a major problem. There was nowhere to tie the rope off to. Kevin Shea had the other end of the rope and was searching frantically for a spot. It didn't do any good because there was nothing up there.

"Now Gallegos was getting ready to go. The flames were too much. In José's mind he was going to die either from the fire or the heat, and he was prepared to jump if he couldn't take the pain. I climbed up on the parapet and put my legs over the side and supported myself with my hands. I didn't think I would have any trouble supporting myself there until Kevin Shea found a spot.

"Shea was a very resourceful firefighter, and I had no doubt he would figure something out, but I have to say I was still pretty surprised when he did. Since there were no pipes or railings or anything else, he did the most natural thing in the world for him. He tied the rope around himself."

"When Paddy Barr started to go over the wall without being tied to anything," remembers Shea, "I knew I was out of time and had to do something right away. I always wore a personal harness, even if I wasn't doing a rescue. I made it so the rescue rope could be fed out to lower him down by using a large D ring that was clipped over my harness. I found a small air-conditioning unit and thought that it might be a possibility. I gave it the ultimate test—I kicked it hard. Unfortunately, some of the cover tore off, so that idea was out. When I saw Barr going over the edge I yelled, 'Not yet!'

"There is a theory in doing these types of rescues that you should only tie off to a bomb-proof spot. That means if a bomb went off, that spot would still be there. In this case, that wasn't going to happen and we were out of time. I was going to have to be that spot. I put the rope through the D ring and held the rope with my hands. Then I sat down on the roof with my feet against the wall."

Barr looked down at Shea and started over the side. Lieutenant Brown was still on the parapet talking to José. He told him not to worry because they were coming down to get him.

"I didn't have a good feeling about going over the side. It wasn't that I didn't trust Kevin Shea, because he and I were held together. If I went, then he was going too. I told Paddy Brown not to let me fall. He told me that wasn't going to happen and not to worry. He had such a wonderful reputation on the FDNY and I felt fine with it after that. I knew he would never tell me something that wasn't so. If I heard those same words from 90 percent of the other officers, it wouldn't mean a thing, but not when Paddy Brown was concerned. He was a real-deal kind of guy.

"That was all I needed to hear and I went over the side. I could hear the construction workers and the people in the street yelling and cheering. I had never heard anything like this before. I was wearing my turnout coat and regular blue pants. As I was being lowered down to him, I was pretty nervous. I told José that we were going to get him out of there. As I got closer to him, I could definitely feel the heat. I was concerned that the room might flash over. I was certain if that happened, he would be blown off the ledge."

Shea slowly fed the rope as Lieutenant Brown monitored Barr's descent. Shea's eyes inspected the wall for any sign of movement. If the parapet gave way, it would have been the end of all of them.

"I had recently come over from Brooklyn, and the parapet walls there were often in terrible shape," recounts Shea. "I had been on roofs that if you pushed on the parapet it would crumble. I kept thinking the whole wall might go and take all of us with it. But everything was going well and none of the brick or mortar was loose. I kept feeding the line out slowly."

The distance that Barr had to travel wasn't great, only about eighteen feet or so. It would have been better if they had a pipe or railing to feed the line over, but there was only the mortar and brick edge, which would not do them any good. As Barr got closer, he began to prepare José Gallegos for what he wanted him to do.

"I told him that I was going to wrap my legs around him and that he was to put his arms around me. I told him not to jump on me; instead I wanted him to let me get to the ledge and stand there for a moment and then we would go down to the floor below. Compounding the problem was the increasing heat and smoke and the fact that José didn't speak much English.

"With that, he leaped straight out and grabbed me. I was absolutely not ready for him. With the language barrier, who knows what he thought I said, plus he was very frightened. When he hit me I grabbed him, but he started to slip away. I wrapped my legs and arms around him and he did the same thing with me and then he was OK. I didn't know what happened above, but the two of us started to free-fall and we were spinning."

When the amount of the weight nearly doubled, Shea shot into the air. Standing nearby, Firefighters Bruce Newberry and O'Keefe dove across him. This brought Shea back down to the surface of the roof. Without their quick action, Shea would probably have been swept over the side, carrying him, Barr, and José Gallegos to their deaths.

After the dropping and spinning stopped, Barr was directly across from a window on the eleventh floor. Firefighters were on that floor waiting for them. With the radio traffic so heavy, they were not aware he had come down already. Barr could do nothing other than punch at the window with his feet to get their attention.

"I was in a spot I couldn't get out of. With Gallegos holding on to me, I couldn't climb onto the ledge. The people in the street below and on the construction site were cheering again, and I was too. They finally saw me and broke out the window and pulled José inside. After they had him inside and safe, they got me. That was totally a team effort. I undid the rope and Kevin pulled it back up.

"After that time, I talked to a lot of the construction workers, and they told me they were certain that José was going to jump. They were yelling to him not to do it because firefighters were coming. They calmed him down to a point where he didn't jump.

"When we got inside, José was nearly in shock. He wasn't burned, but he had suffered some effects of smoke inhalation. I stayed with him and walked him down to the ambulance."

FDNY procedures call for a rope to be taken out of service following such a rescue because it must be inspected for damage. This was especially true for a rope that had been through the abrasion this one had. Until it passed inspection, it was considered to be condemned and not fit for use.

The fire on the twelfth floor was definitely not under control. Firefighters from the engine company had gained entrance to the floor and began to conduct a search for others who might be trapped. One firefighter became disoriented in the smoke and fire and had to be rescued himself.

After they got Barr inside, Shea pulled the rope back up. "I knew we weren't done yet. When I first got up on the roof, I looked over the edge and saw another man on the ledge on the other side of the building. He had been driven out by the fire, but José Gallegos was in greater imminent danger than the second man, Peter Lewis.

"We only had one rope, and that one was considered condemned. That may have been so, but there was a man on a ledge who was facing death and I knew I had to go down and get him. I couldn't wait. I was afraid that Lewis wouldn't last until we got another rope. Besides that, there was the heat. The rescue rope was made of nylon and it would not tolerate heat very well.

"As soon as I had the rope back, I tied it into my rescue belt. Rescue 1 Firefighter Ray McCormick fed the rope through his rescue belt the same way I had previously done. He sat down on the roof just as I had done. Lieutenant Brown was on the parapet just as he had been with Paddy Barr. I told Peter Lewis to hold on, and that I would be down to get him in a moment. He looked back into the room and told me to hurry up.

"I went over the side and Ray McCormick fed the rope out slowly, and I was down to the ledge in a matter of a minute. I knew I didn't want this guy to jump onto me like Gallegos had done with Paddy. He was a good-sized guy and I was afraid I wouldn't be able to hold him."

As Shea was being lowered down, Firefighter McCormick sat on the roof with his legs against the parapet. Firefighters O'Keefe and Newberry lay on top of him. They weren't taking any chances after what happened with Barr.

"When I got even with the ledge, I was able to step on it. I told him I wanted him to put his arms around my neck and wrap his legs around my waist. While I talked to him, I could see over his shoulder that the fire was coming over the top of the door, and I knew we didn't have much time. I told him it was time to go. He climbed on me just like I asked him to do, and I stepped off the ledge. There were no drops in the rope or any surging down."

On the parapet, Lieutenant Brown gave directions to McCormick, who again started feeding the line out. Slowly, Shea continued to descend to the eleventh floor. Unlike Barr, he was not wearing his turnout coat. It was a hot day, and he had removed it when he got to the roof. Shea didn't think the coat would be much use if the fire came out the window as it would have burned the nylon rope in two anyway.

"There was a bit of a distraction with the firefighters on the eleventh floor. There had been a distress call from a firefighter fighting the fire, and some of them had left to go help him. Those remaining seemed rather shocked to see me coming down, but when they saw us they pulled us both onto the ledge.

"As soon as we got inside, Lewis started coughing. He had breathed in a lot of smoke. He asked me if he was going to be all right because of everything he was coughing up. I could see that he was really frightened and I told him it was very normal.

"The fire situation was not getting better above so once I knew he was going to be all right I wanted to go back up and help out. One of the firefighters was suffering from heat exhaustion and had taken off his turnout gear. I put it on and went back to the twelfth floor to the fire."

Patrick Barr and Kevin Shea were honored for their heroic actions by *Firehouse* magazine as part of their Heroism and Community Service program. Both of them received the equivalent of Medals of Valor from the Fire Department of the city of New York, with Barr being awarded the Emily Trevor/Mary B. Warren Medal and Shea the Hugh Bonner Medal.

When asked by a reporter to reflect on that day, Barr's droll wit came through when he remarked, "It wasn't just another day at the office." When asked if they believed that they were heroes, Barr said, "They are calling me a hero, but I don't see it." Gesturing to his whole crew he added, "It's the guys I work with, we're a team." As for Shea, he also said no to the label of hero. "I was just there. I was lucky; any one of my crew would have done it. It was just my turn to go."

Both firefighters have since retired from the FDNY. Kevin Shea was forced to retire as a result of injuries he suffered in a five-story fall in 1993, after the first attack on the World Trade Center. Patrick Barr, an FDNY heavyweight boxing champion, served for more than twenty years, and he too has retired.

In a sad postscript to the heroic team effort on Seventh Avenue, Lieutenant Patrick Brown, Patrick O'Keefe, and Kevin Dowdell all perished on September 11, 2001.

23

THE SANCTUARY THAT WASN'T

January 28, 1994

Philadelphia, Pennsylvania

Louis Brasten, Stith Claiborne, Fred Endrikat

In 1846, an Episcopal church was built in the city of Philadelphia, on Twelfth Street between Catharine and Fitzwater Streets. By 1994, it had been sold twice and in its most recent incarnation had become the Rising Sun Baptist Church. Built of fieldstone in the traditional form of a cross, it was a stately building standing nearly four stories tall. Nine lancet-type windows were along the rear of the church. They were twelve inches wide and more than five feet tall at their pointed top and were filled with old stained glass.

The morning of January 28, 1994, was a busy one for the Philadelphia Fire Department. An ice storm had hit the city a few days earlier, but then the temperature rose to a rainy fifty-nine degrees, which was the warmest temperature ever recorded on that day. The rain and unseasonable temperature had not slowed things down.

Left to right: Stith Claiborne, Louis Brasten, and Fred Endrikat of the Philadelphia Fire Department stand at attention as the casket carrying the body of Vencent Acey passes them.

Rescue 1 had started its day at eight in the morning, and by noon they had been on six calls. At 12:16 P.M., a 911 call came in reporting a fire at the beautiful old church. Engine 1 was first on the scene. Lieutenant John McKleer and Firefighter Walter Jackson were let into the church by one of the deacons. A light amount of smoke came from the rear of the church.

It seemed that the fire's source might be at the back of the church, but when they got back there, no fire was found. A trapdoor was in the floor of one of the administrative offices at the rear, and it was the only way to get into the basement. The two men opened it up and smoke came out. The lieutenant wanted Jackson to check the basement for fire, so he pulled an inch-and-three-quarter preconnect hose line from the engine and proceeded down the narrow and quite steep wooden stairs.

"When we got the door open, there was a lot of heat and smoke coming up. I was wearing full turnouts, and I had my Nomex hood on and my SCBA," remembers Jackson. "Once I got down there, I couldn't see a thing. We advanced our line in as far as we could, but we couldn't find the fire and we were certain one was in there.

"After about fifteen minutes of searching the basement, my warning alarm on my SCBA went off, and I had to get a new bottle. When I came up, I saw our lieutenant and said, 'Hey Loo, we have heavy smoke and heat down there.' After I got my replacement bottle, I went back down again and we continued looking in the ceiling for the fire. We knew it couldn't be far away."

Lieutenant Fred Endrikat and Firefighters Stith Claiborne, Vencent Acey, James Kelly, Joseph Murray, and Michael Pateski were also on Rescue 1's truck that day. In addition to Engine 1, several other companies from the initial fire alarm were at the fire. Firefighter Louis Brasten was another member of Rescue 1, but he was detailed to Engine Company 13's Air Unit 1 that day. On citywide working fires, Engine 13 was dispatched with Air Unit 1, who carried extra SCBA air bottles and an onboard air compressor to refill them.

Rescue 1 was ordered to proceed to the back of the church on Sartain Street and assist Engine 3. The firefighters of Rescue 1 pulled a hose line from a nearby hydrant and then made forcible entry and began ventilating the rear of the building. Lieutenant Endrikat broke his team down into three groups—Claiborne and Acey were the roof team; Kelly and Murray were the search team, with the lieutenant and the driver, Michael Pateski, augmenting them. Medium to heavy smoke conditions were observed at the back of the church with no evidence of fire.

At this early point in the fire, fire-ground tactics did not require the opening up of the main roof of the church for ventilation. So Acey and Claiborne used power saws with metal-cutting blades to open up the iron fence and grating, which would facilitate access to the fire-ground area for the other firefighters. Claiborne said to Acey, "Let's go around and see if we can help somebody else." They made an entrance at the front side of the church, and they encountered some of the firefighters who had been in the basement area trying to locate the fire. Their SCBAs were running low, and they were coming out to change bottles.

"Acey and I were going in to relieve some of the firefighters who needed to get new air bottles. We knew the fire was in the back of the church, and we relieved them on their hose line for a while. The smoke was very thick, a heavy black kind.

"Acey and I followed the inch-and-three-quarter hose that had been pulled by Engine 1. It went back to the rear of the church and into a small office. We still hadn't seen any fire, which was very unusual. A trapdoor that led to a basement was in that room. We didn't know about the basement until we saw the trapdoor. We followed the line back toward where the nozzle was located.

"When we found the tip, it was shut off, and there wasn't anyone there. We started looking for the fire. We knew it was in the back of the building, but we couldn't see any fire because the heavy, black smoke prevented us from seeing anything. We opened up the nozzle and began to spray in the direction of the heat."

During this time, Lieutenant Endrikat was working on the second floor. He knew the fire was in the walls of the old church. "We opened up the walls upstairs to try to attack the fire. The problem we faced was how the fire was able to move upward and burn rapidly at a very high temperature. The church had an outer wall, dead-air space, and an inner wall. The fire was growing in that dead-air space, but we had no idea how fast.

"I had been in contact with Stith Claiborne via our portable radios, and I knew he and Acey were working an inch-and-three-quarter line in the basement. The last word I got from them was that they were all right and moving in.

"Conditions began to change rapidly on the second floor. I was with Firefighter Jim Kelly and we continued to open the walls up. The more we opened them up, the greater the heat was. I didn't have a good feeling about the situation because it was changing way too fast. Then we started to hear a strange sound."

Claiborne and Acey continued to play water into the rear area of the basement and advanced cautiously in an effort to locate and attack the source of the basement heat and smoke. "There was a lot of noise in there, and I thought my SCBA was low, but I couldn't hear the alarm if it went off," said Claiborne. "It was impossible to tell the condition of my tank because the smoke was so black and it was banked down to the floor. I told Acey that I was going outside to check it out and that I would be right back. It was very difficult to find my way out, as my vision was zero. I moved out and saw that I had almost a quarter-tank left."

Endrikat listened to the sounds coming from the walls. "It was a crackling sound—that of a fire that had taken hold and yet was invisible to us. The result of this invisible fire was to drive the temperature up to a point where a flashover was becoming a real threat. Up to that point, I didn't think that we would switch from an offensive interior attack to a defensive position, but we had to. After receiving information from fire officers inside the church, an order to evacuate the building was given by the deputy chief in charge of the fire ground. Using my radio, I contacted Stith again. I could sense something different in his voice. Not a panic or a Mayday type of tone, but something definitely was wrong. At that time, we had difficulty exiting the sanctuary area of the second floor of the church because of tremendous heat and smoke conditions."

In almost an instant, conditions had deteriorated throughout the building, especially in the first-floor area where Claiborne was now located. "I could see that the fire was changing and I didn't like it," Claiborne remembers. "I noticed the smoke that had been coming out of the side door of the church was now curling around and being sucked back in. This meant that the fire was growing rapidly, and it was demanding more oxygen and getting it. I knew I had to radio Acey and tell him and anyone else what was going on and to get out.

"I would have had to walk about a block and a half to get another SCBA bottle, so I decided not to change my air bottle. I had enough to go back in, get Acey, and tell him to get out. I took out my personal search rope and tied it to a downspout near the entry door on the first floor. I told all the firefighters I encountered not to mess with the rope. If something happened, this was going to be the rope that Vence and I would follow back to escape the building. The smoke was building to such a condition that it was nearly impossible to see. Lieutenant Endrikat had taught me about the search rope and how important it was to always use it when you entered an unfamiliar area, especially in a large building. I remember his words, 'Stith, this rope can save your life.'

"I got back to the stairs and started down. Just then came a tremendous 'whoooofff' sound and all hell broke loose. The whole place flashed over, and burning debris fell down on me. I turned around and began to move back up as fast as I could. I yelled into my radio, 'Vence, get out of there! Vence, get out of there! Vence, get out of there!'

"I wasn't familiar with the layout, and it was pitch-black. The hose lines were a twisted mess. I fell over them several times, and at one point, I went down pretty hard and lost my helmet. When I came out, my coat and hair were smoking and I was close to catching on fire. Outside, I just lay there and collected myself. I knew I had come close to not making it back out.

"The only way I ever got out was by following my search rope. I didn't know it then, but one of the guys from Ladder 11, Sam Marks, later said the only way he and some others got out was by following my search rope too."

The whole back of the church had flashed over, trapping several other firefighters, including Captain Jim O'Donnell from Engine 11 and Walter Jackson. The hot gases in the basement ignited when those on the first floor caught fire, continuing the massive flashover. Acey dropped his hose and moved back toward the stairway. He climbed onto the first floor and began to make his way to the exit.

Firefighter Louis Brasten was at the rear of the church, on the Sartain Street side. "We had been ventilating the lancet window. Suddenly, a roar came from inside the church. The first floor was filled with flame that came blowing out. There were firefighters on the other side who were burning. I had an ax, and I started whaling away on the wooden casements, breaking them open to make a larger opening for them to get out. I could hear them calling for help in there, and we were doing the best we could to get them the opening they needed. It seems ironic that they were trapped in a place called the 'sanctuary.' "

A drop ceiling near the administrative offices in the back of the church created about four feet of dead air space. The fire that developed in the walls fed hot gases into that space. When these gases reached the point of ignition, they exploded, starting the huge flashover. In the process, it propelled the false ceiling down on the firefighters.

Lieutenant Endrikat found his way out of the second-floor sanctuary and exited the building. He came out a side door into a courtyard and saw Claiborne. "He was on his hands and knees in an exterior doorway in the first floor rear of the church. His helmet was missing and heavy fire was venting over his head at the top of the doorway."

Firefighters came up to Claiborne and asked him what was wrong. "I told them there were a lot of guys still in there. I told them about Vence Acey being in the basement, and I remembered when I was coming up to check my SCBA that another firefighter was going down the stairs. I didn't know who it was because I couldn't see anything.

"I knew we were going back in there, but I was out of air and I needed a helmet. I went and got another SCBA and found a helmet. Then I ran back to the door and went in again."

Lieutenant Endrikat received word about more trapped firefighters from Battalion 4's Acting Battalion Chief John Weres. "John told me that Captain Jim O'Donnell was trapped in the same area where Stith had escaped from. Sam Marks from Ladder 11, Jimmy Kelly, and I had a hose line that Kelly had relocated, and we went back in to search for Jim O'Donnell."

Walter Jackson, who was talking with Captain O'Donnell when the room exploded, was also trapped. "The smoke was very heavy already, but the heat was really growing. The captain told us to clear the building, and we were just starting out. I don't think I even took a couple of steps and everything was red. The heat was tremendous, and I knew I was burning and bad. The ceiling blew down on us. I tried to get up, but I couldn't. I was lying on the floor under pieces of ceiling and I thought I heard a low-air alarm, but it seemed far away. Then, there wasn't any more air. I crawled toward the windows, but I don't remember doing it. I just remember lying there and then Fred was there."

Firefighter Kelly was on the hose tip as the three firefighters made their way to their fallen comrades. Claiborne searched for his partner behind them. Kelly sprayed the hose back and forth down a hallway as they advanced to the first floor, where Captain O'Donnell was trapped. Soon, they were at the door of the room that contained the trapdoor to the basement. Endrikat entered and followed the wall to his right. He found one helmet, then another.

"When we got to the doorway, the hose line got hung up and could not be advanced any farther. Sam Marks and Jim Kelly held their position, and I went into the room. Even though I was going in there, in reality it was all three of us because there is no way I could have done it alone. They were my protection and made it possible for me to get in there. As soon as I got in and found the helmets," Endrikat remembers, "I felt something under the rubble on the floor. The room was a mess following the flashover. I lifted a piece of the debris and there was Captain O'Donnell. I grabbed him and pulled him up. I shined my light in his face and saw that he was unconscious. It was obvious that he was severely burned and there wasn't much time. I removed my mask and placed it over Jim's face, hoping to give him enough air to be able to get out of there. The room suddenly got extremely hot, and I thought it was going to flash over again. I could feel myself getting burned. I found out later that Kelly had directed the hose-line stream at the ceiling directly over where Jim and I were to knock down the heavy fire overhead. When the bulk of the fire was knocked down, Kelly and Marks immediately came into the room to help with Captain O'Donnell. We moved him over to the narrow rear window. We got his SCBA off and got him through the window. Louis Brasten was on the outside, and he helped pull the captain to safety.

"When I found two helmets I thought we might find other firefighters in that room, but didn't know who. And then we found Walter Jackson. He was very close to the window. I had no idea he was in there. We got his SCBA off and picked him up. He was semiconscious, and we got him to a rear window where Louis Brasten and other firefighters outside helped pull him to safety."

Claiborne entered the first-floor rear hallway of the church after Endrikat, Kelly, and Marks had cleared a path with the hose. It was now easier for him to gain entrance to the area for the third time. Crawling along and feeling as he went, Claiborne didn't want to miss anything. Then he found something.

"I hit something as I was going along. I looked closely and it was a boot. Feeling more closely I realized I had found Vence Acey. He nearly made it all the way out. Another firefighter, Charlie Grover, was searching nearby. I asked him for help getting Vence to safety. The two of us worked as fast and hard as we could. It took us about three minutes to do the job. Vence was lifeless, which made it harder.

"The paramedics were out in the courtyard and we turned Vence over to them. As I pulled him the last part of the way, I looked closely at my friend, and I knew then that he was gone. The fire had killed Vence Acey. There would be plenty of time to take in what had just happened, but for now there were other firefighters to worry about."

As soon as the last firefighter was rescued from the first floor, Brasten ran around to the side of the building. An SCBA was lying in the courtyard. He put it on and entered the church to help his Rescue 1 crew members. Just before he entered, he saw the paramedics working on Vence Acey.

"When I saw them working on Vence, I knew he must be in bad shape," remembers Brasten. "I didn't know he had been killed at that time. I went in and met up with Deputy Chief Robert Wauhop. That was when we learned that another firefighter was still missing.

"The chief told us that they believed John Redmond from Ladder 11 was last seen in the basement. He told us to form a team and make a sweep of the first floor. We got Lieutenant Mike Yeager from Engine 68 to go with us. Chief Wauhop looked us in the eyes and told us not to go into the basement.

"When we got into the first floor, it was heavily involved in fire. Fred and I were on our hands and knees. I went to the right and Fred went left, sweeping the floor as we went. Normally, a firefighter's PASS alarm would lead us to them, but there was a tremendous amount of noise in that area. When the firefighters dropped their SCBAs, their alarms went off. You can't easily shut one off and so they contributed to the confusion. In addition to the alarms was the sound of the fire that roared above us.

"We searched that room and found several SCBAs and helmets but no downed firefighters. John Redmond was still unaccounted for, and the only place we hadn't checked was the basement. I knew the chief told us not to go down there, but I felt that since we had searched the area we were assigned to with a negative result, he would want us to go into the basement.

"The obvious danger to entering the basement was that there was only one way in, one way out, and a fire raging above and around us. If the building collapsed, we would have been in serious trouble. That was one side of the situation. The other was that we had come to the fire with John and now he was missing. We weren't leaving without him. I told Fred I wanted to go down to the basement and he agreed that we had to do it."

Lieutenant Yeager stayed above, directing that area of the rescue operation. In a couple of minutes, Firefighters Michael Pateski, James

Kelly, and Samuel Marks joined him with a hose line. They knew the hopes of rescuing their lost friend rested with Brasten and Endrikat. At the same time, the fate of those two rested in the hands of the four fire-fighters who were fighting to keep the fire from collapsing any more of the structure. If it did, it could effectively trap the rescuers in a fiery basement tomb. And the four knew their own fate rested on how well they did their jobs. If there was any type of collapse, they would be the first to know it, and it might be the last thing they would ever know. Endrikat and Brasten then descended the stairs.

"The first thing we did was hook ourselves up to a search rope," Brasten explains. "I hadn't been down there, and I wasn't sure if it was an open space or another maze of rooms we would have to navigate with zero visibility. We made our way to the bottom of the stairs and started a search. There were six to eight inches of water on the floor, and it was rising steadily.

"I followed the inch-and-three-quarter hose line to the end. I swept my hands out as I went. Endrikat was right behind me. We stayed together on this search. When I got to the end of the hose, the tip was closed and there was no sign of Redmond. I went another five or ten feet beyond the tip, going in the same general direction. I continued to spread my hands out in front of me and to the side as I went. Then I hit something. I felt a boot.

"It was John Redmond. His mask was off and he was lying facedown in the water. I pulled him up to me and checked to see if he was breathing. He wasn't. I pulled off my air mask and cleared out John's mouth. Then I started to perform CPR on him. I did this for a couple of minutes before I had to stop.

"I couldn't breathe the air down there. I knew if I continued without my own mask, I would lose consciousness. Fred was right with me and could tell I was having trouble breathing. I said to him that we had to get John out as soon as possible. Then I gave him one more breath before I pulled my own mask back on."

Following their search rope, they pulled their comrade back to the steps. Both of them proceeded to lift the limp body of John Redmond up the stairs. As they did this, he became wedged in the narrow stairwell around the third or fourth tread. At this point, Brasten ran out of air.

"My low-air bell had started to sound just after we got into the basement, but I couldn't turn back then. We were close to finding John and I had to stay. It was a different matter now. I was empty and when I breathed in, I just sucked the mask to my face. I had to get another bottle. The air in there was just too bad to survive without it, let alone having to use all my strength to help get John up the stairs. As it was, he felt like he weighed a thousand pounds.

"I told Fred I was going to get another pack from one of the guys at the top of the stairs. I climbed up and told Mike Yeager that I needed his SCBA. He dropped it immediately and I put it on. I started back down the steps and I could see that Fred was in trouble."

The lieutenant was indeed having difficulty. A tremendous amount of water was being put on the fire, and most of it had ended up in the basement. The hot water was about five feet deep, and at that point, drowning became a consideration.

Lieutenant Endrikat had asked for a rope to secure Redmond. It would subsequently be used to lift him from the basement. After Endrikat made a harness out of the rope, he called for the firefighters at the top of the steps to put tension on it. Claiborne had returned to the top of the stairs and assisted Lieutenant Yeager, who stayed on even without an SCBA. As they were pulling the rope tight, Lieutenant Endrikat's mask was ripped from his face. He became hopelessly tangled in the rope, and he fell off the stairwell into the chest-high water. After he released the buckles on his SCBA harness and let it fall away into the water, he began to breathe the incredibly toxic mixture of gases in the basement.

Louis Brasten came to his aid. "When I saw he was in trouble, I started down to get to him. With no warning, I fell and then I was jolted to a stop as my chest hit a large beam. It fractured my sternum and took the air right out of my lungs. I grabbed onto a vertical beam and pulled myself up. It took a few seconds to get my bearings again. No matter what happened to me, I had to make sure Fred was all right. I got back to where they were, straddling both Endrikat and Redmond. I told the

guys above us that we would push while they pulled. I then realized
something was wrong with one of my eyes. I didn't know it then, but I
had cut my cornea at some point, perhaps in the fall."

Then, as Lieutenant Endrikat held John Redmond's head above the
water, a tremendous roar came. "A nearby section of the church collapsed," recalls Endrikat. "It was getting hard for me to concentrate
then, and I was having a hard time breathing as well. Then more of the
building fell. I remember just closing my eyes, and the only thing I could
think of was my wife and children. At that point I really didn't know if
we were going to get out of there. It didn't look too good."

But Yeager and Claiborne held the rope. Marks, Pateski, and Kelly
stood their ground against the fire and kept a steady stream of water
playing on the flames only a few feet above them. None flinched as the
thunderous collapses occurred, and because of that, Redmond was
pulled from the stairs. Endrikat, who was barely conscious, was pulled
up and, with his arm around another firefighter's neck, made his way to
the courtyard. Brasten was fighting exhaustion but exited under his own
power. A waiting paramedic unit transported Endrikat and Brasten to
Hahneman Hospital.

The remaining firefighters carried John Redmond to daylight, but the
light was gone for him. What Endrikat and Brasten couldn't bear to consider had come to pass. The man they had all fought so hard to save was
gone.

In the emergency room, Fire Commissioner Harold Hairston came
to check on his firefighters. He and Lieutenant Endrikat talked. "I asked
him about Jimmy O'Donnell. Jim and I were previously assigned as lieutenants to Engine 45 together and were good friends. He told me he was
in a burn center in critical but stable condition. He said that Walter Jackson was in the same condition as well. Then, he hit me with news that
devastated me. Vence Acey and John Redmond were both gone.

"I don't remember much of the conversation after that. I know I had
smoke inhalation and first- and second-degree burns on my face, neck,
and ears and that they had treated me, but I don't remember anything
else except I wanted to go home and be with my wife and children."

Walter Jackson remained in critical condition for five and a half weeks. He suffered second- and third-degree burns over much of his body, including burns to his lungs. He has undergone seven operations to repair the damage caused by that fire. "I live with that fire every time I look in the mirror. Even so, I am not sorry I was there. I was lucky to be there, to have a chance to help others. With everything that happened to me, it felt good to be there and help." He was decorated with the Heroism Award from the International Association of Firefighters Local 22. It took a long time, but he made it back to work and continues his career as a firefighter. James O'Donnell returned to full duty and has subsequently retired.

Lieutenant Endrikat remembers the first time he saw Walter Jackson after he was released from the hospital. "I was working in my office at Rescue 1. I heard a knock and the door opened. There stood Walter Jackson. I really can't express the mixed emotions that I felt when I saw Walt and how badly burned he was. I was humbled by what Jackson told me next. He had come to thank me, Jim Kelly, and Sam Marks for saving his life that day. It felt like a victory from a day that didn't have many."

For their heroic actions on the fire ground at the Rising Sun Baptist Church that day, Lieutenant Fred Endrikat and Firefighter Louis Brasten were each awarded the Philadelphia Fire Department's highest award for heroism. Firefighter Stith Claiborne received the Philadelphia Fire Department's Merit Award, the second-highest award for bravery. In addition, Brasten and Endrikat were decorated for their heroism by the Ancient Order of the Hibernians, each receiving the Hibernian Medal. *Firehouse* magazine awarded a Medal for Valor as part of their national Heroism and Community Service Award program to Lieutenant Endrikat and Firefighters Brasten and Claiborne.

In looking back on the Rising Sun Baptist Church fire, Brasten remembers trying to explain to Delores and Michael Redmond how and why their son died. "His mom didn't understand why he died. 'There weren't any people to rescue that day, why did he have to die?' I told her

I thought both he and Vencent Acey did rescue other people—firefighters. When they held their position in the basement and continued to put water on the source of the fire, it afforded a lot of other firefighters a chance to escape when the building flashed over. If they hadn't held their position so valiantly, it was highly probable that when the building flashed over it would have been much more severe and would have likely taken more lives. It was a small gesture, but I felt it was important for them to know the kind of firefighter and, more importantly, the man their son was."

After the fire is put out and the burns heal and perhaps loved ones are buried, sometimes the experience isn't over and won't ever be. For Rescue 1 Lieutenant Fred Endrikat, there "isn't a day that goes by when I wake up that my first thoughts aren't of John and Vence. I have gone over everything that happened that day a thousand times. What could I have done to make things different?

"As far as the medals go, it made me extremely uncomfortable being decorated. It is impossible for me to consider those awards as an individual accomplishment. Firefighting is not about individual achievements; it's about teamwork. I still believe that the awards don't really belong to me, they belong to the firefighters on that fire ground; they belong to the Philadelphia Fire Department, and in particular, they especially belong to the other guys in Rescue 1. It is even more uncomfortable to receive awards when one of my men died that day. It was my responsibility to bring him back safely and I didn't do it. Those medals serve as a reminder of my failings that day."

When Lieutenant Endrikat's oldest daughter applied for college five years after the fire, she was required to write an essay and include a photograph with it about a subject that had a significant impact on her life. She submitted a photograph of a Philadelphia Fire Department truck with the flag-draped coffin of Vencent Acey. Fred Endrikat, Louis Brasten, and Stith Claiborne are also in the picture. She wrote about the church fire and talked about how it had changed her father, and how that change had affected her relationship with him. There was a time when he played and laughed with her, kidded around, and was always light-hearted. But those were the days before they went to the awful fire ground at the Rising Sun Baptist Church.

When asked if things have returned to normal, Lieutenant Endrikat replied, "To a degree, but it will never be like it was before. But whatever we feel is only a fraction of the heartache the families of Vencent Acey and John Redmond live with every day. I can't imagine how painful it is for those families, especially the children.

"I hope the legacy of that fire will be in small things, like teaching young firefighters to always be prepared, in teaching them when and how to use search ropes, and in never accepting a level of commitment that is less than everything you have inside you.

"If I could change one thing in my entire life, it would be the results of that day."

24

THIRTY-EIGHT MINUTES

May 23, 1997

Portland, Oregon

Don Beahm, Daniel Hershey, Wes Loucks, Bruce Thompson

Firefighters talk about "fuel load" in gauging the danger of a structure and its contents. The measure of combustibility and hazardousness of the materials housed in a certain building greatly influences the dangers of a fuel load, and it is hard to imagine any building with a greater load than Bargains Galore. The company sold salvage paper goods—four floors of combustible material. While working a standard inventory and sorting through saleable items, employees used a trash chute on the outside of the building, which led to a dumpster. Inventory was tedious but simple: trash went down the chute, while saleable items were transferred to the first floor of the buiding.

At 9:10 A.M., seventeen-year-old Dylan Burke finished loading three pallets of paper supplies onto the freight elevator and punched the button for the first floor. Pulling down the wooden safety gate, he began his

**The Bargains Galore paper goods store is blazing as firefighters
work to rescue employee Dylan Burke.**

descent. Just before the elevator reached the second floor, the lights in the building flickered a few times and the elevator stopped for a moment.

Burke was relieved a second or two later when the lights came back on and the antiquated elevator resumed its travel. He was now past the second floor when again the lights flickered and then went out. Thinking it would be as before, he waited—nothing. He tried to pry open the door to escape, but was unable to open it.

Then came shouting from inside the building. His coworkers had been told to abandon Bargains Galore. The building was on fire and Burke was trapped.

Across town, the call came in to Portland Fire Department's heavy rescue squad. The unit was formed to handle specialty and highly technical rescues. All fire companies carry the equipment to save people from burning structures, but sometimes specialized equipment is needed to accomplish the rescue. Squad 1 carried the tools and was trained constantly for heavy fuel load situations. This was a day they were prepared for.

Firefighters Don Beahm, Bruce Thompson, Daniel Hershey, and Acting Lieutenant Wes Loucks were about to face the impossible. With every tick of the clock, the fire grew and the temperature inside the building rose.

At the same time the employees abandoned the building, Fire Inspector Gary Boyles happened to be driving past the warehouse and saw the fire. He stopped and talked to the crowd of employees and learned that Dylan was still inside. Without protective gear, Boyles and the young man's stepfather ran into the building to find him.

"Help me! Get me out of here!" Boyles heard a faint voice calling. Over and over Dylan called. Each call brought the inspector closer to him. When Boyles got to the second floor, he finally found what he was looking for—and more. The young man was inside the elevator and the flames were closing in.

As Squad 1 crossed the Willamette River, the firefighters could see their destination. There was no question about what they had. This was a big fire.

First Boyles tried to pull the elevator doors open, but to no avail. Then he used a piece of wood in an attempt to pry the doors open—that didn't work either. Boyles told Dylan he was going for help. With the smoke and confusion caused by all the pallets stacked everywhere he was unable to find the stairwell, but was able to locate a window. He saw the first trucks arriving and yelled out the window to them, explaining Dylan's location and situation.

As he finished talking, a ball of fire shot across the ceiling, driving Boyles out to the fire escape. Flames were consuming the second floor and going back in to help was not an option. In order to save himself, he had to abandon his position, and he dropped about fifteen feet to the ground.

Engine Companies 1, 3, 4, 23, and 24, along with Truck 4, pulled up to the building one after the other. Their mission was clear. They were charged with attacking the fire. In this case, they would also try to prevent a young man from burning to death while four firefighters from Squad 1 worked to make his extrication possible.

Don Beahm was the driver of the heavy rescue truck. As soon as they pulled up, Bruce Thompson, Dan Hershey, and Wes Loucks entered the building while Beahm put on his turnout gear and pulled on an SCBA. Thompson and Hershey found that when the power failed, the elevator had been caught between floors and thus the doors were prohibited from opening by safety systems. The two firefighters tried to gain entrance to the elevator but were unsuccessful.

Don Beahm's wife, Debbie, also a fire captain in another town, had just gotten the children off to school when a news bulletin flashed across the screen. They were going live to a large fire at a warehouse in downtown Portland. "When I saw Squad 1's heavy rescue rig parked at the front door of the building, I knew Don was there. I could see the faces on the firefighters and they had a look that cut right into me. I knew from their expressions that they were worried. I couldn't see Don or any of the rest of Squad 1, so I knew they were inside a building that was fully involved in flames. Even though I know how good Don and his squad are, I was scared."

The four firefighters determined that the elevator was not powered with cables, but instead was a hydraulic elevator, meaning it operated by means of water. The rescuers used the Hurst Tool (Jaws of Life) to pry the doors open. The doors opened easily but no one could get through the flames to Dylan. They needed the elevator to move.

Beahm and Thompson went below to look at the equipment in an effort to understand how the system worked. By then the flames had completely consumed the third and fourth floors, and were in almost total control of the second. They couldn't cut through the floor to effect an escape, as it was a massive steel plate suspended two stories up from the elevator pit in the basement. Beahm was convinced that the only way to lower the elevator was by releasing the pressure on the hydraulic lines. That could take an hour or more to accomplish—they had only minutes.

Monitoring the progress outside of the building was Chief Ed Wilson. He and Deputy Chief Delmar Stevens were very concerned about the stability of the building. As the fire overtook the structure, the possibility of a collapse increased substantially. They knew there was a victim trapped inside and a rescue attempt underway, but they also had many firefighters' lives to consider. It would be painful to evacuate, but if it came to saving their firefighters, that was what they would do.

Flames were now encircling the elevator. Dylan used the combustible paper products and cardboard to cover himself up. He was frantically trying to save his own life. It didn't matter to him if they caught fire or not. Without something, anything, between him and the flames he was going to burn.

Hershey and Loucks knew they were not going to be able to go to Dylan. The only way he was going to live was if they brought him down to them—but the flames were closing in. Loucks remembered, "We were really running out of time. Dan and I decided to put a stream of water up the shaft, between the walls and the elevator. There wasn't anything else we could do right then. That water kept the paper and cardboard Dylan covered himself up with from burning."

Every floor above the first was completely consumed by fire. On the second floor, a firefighter did something that was rarely done. He abandoned his hose and went out the window in a desperate effort to save his life. Chief Wilson had seen enough. Beahm and Thompson were in the basement when they heard the three blasts on the air horn that meant it was time to go. The building had to be evacuated for the safety of the firefighters.

Chief Wilson didn't make the decision lightly. "We never leave anyone behind unless it means certain loss of lives, and that was what I felt we were confronted with that day. Inside the building, Don Beahm felt they were still all right and wanted his crew of four to continue on. I was pretty nervous, but I deferred to him and we took everyone else out. I gave them five more minutes."

Loucks and Beahm both felt there was no reason to leave the building just then. They had a mission that was uncompleted and the only way they would leave was if conditions forced them out. Loucks remembered, "If the heat or flames got to us that was one thing, but we couldn't leave that kid in there. We were his only hope and all of us were going to stick it out, and we were glad the chief gave us the leeway."

Debbie Beahm describes her husband as someone who can figure out what makes things work. If something is broken, he will analyze it and more often than not, make it functional again. At Bargains Galore, Don was going to have to figure out how to make the elevator come down without electricity.

"Thompson and I went down to the basement. Earlier, when I looked down the shaft, I could see a pipe going from the elevator piston assembly and through a wall. I thought we would find the equipment room for the elevator in that room, and we did. It was pretty smoky down there, but we located a room that was closed off with a wire cage–like door. We went in and there was all of the hydraulic gear.

"At first we tried to find a valve to open up, but there wasn't one. Because we were in the basement, we didn't have good communications with the floor above us. I then looked at the pipes and tried to figure out which one would be the right one to break. It would have been great if we had something to cut with, but all we had were our fire axes. That was when we heard the all-clear sound—we just kept working."

Beahm picked out a likely pipe and started swinging away at it. He reasoned that if he was able to bleed off the hydraulic fluid, the elevator would come down. Neither of them knew just how desperate the situation was on the first floor as they worked. One by one, Beahm smashed the heavy steel pipes. Each time one broke, more hydraulic fluid sprayed into the room and they would call up to Loucks and Hershey to see if the elevator was moving. Every time the answer was the same—no. Hershey's SCBA low-air alarm went off and he went outside to get a new bottle.

There was one more pipe that might do the trick, and Beahm started smashing it. He was starting to run out of gas, but he had to keep going. "My ax was nearly destroyed by then and I still hadn't cut through. I finally couldn't do any more—I was there. Bruce Thompson could see what was happening to me and stepped in."

With every bit of muscle in his six-foot, five-inch frame, he plowed his ax into the pipe. One blow—nothing. A second—nothing. Bruce drew his ax back and with the pointed end came down again on the pipe, and fluid went everywhere.

"Almost immediately the firefighters above us were yelling, 'He's coming down, he's coming down.' I didn't know if all that hydraulic oil would burn, but if it did we would have been finished because we were wading in it. We were done there, it was time to leave."

On the first floor, other firefighters had gathered by the elevator. The car was creeping down toward the open doors. Loucks and Hershey had already devised a plan to snatch Dylan off as he went past. Fortunately, the elevator was not descending too rapidly. They knew they had one chance to get him. If he got hung up as they extracted him, he would be crushed against the car and the door.

Thirty-eight minutes had elapsed as the car came to the opening. A collective tug, and Dylan was freed from a fiery tomb. All of the firefighters ran from the building. It was a miracle—no one had been hurt. Not long after the teenager was freed from Bargains Galore, the ceiling collapsed onto the fourth floor, which started the pancake process that eventually led to the whole interior of the building coming to rest on the first floor and the basement.

As Chief Wilson saw the firefighters run from the building with Dylan, he looked at his watch. It had been exactly five minutes. Debbie Beahm was still watching television as her husband came out. She smiled, knowing he was right in the middle of the action, but he was all right.

All of the firefighters present at the Bargains Galore fire ground had a part in saving a life that day. While a few firefighters got the majority of the attention, it was common knowledge that the rescue was carried out by everyone there.

Firefighters Don Beahm, Bruce Thompson, and Daniel Hershey, along with Acting Lieutenant Wes Loucks, were all awarded Portland Fire Department's David Campbell Memorial Association Silver Medal Award for Valor for putting their own lives at considerable risk to save that of another. They also each received the State of Oregon EMS Medal of Valor and the Portland Fire Bureau Silver Medal of Valor.

The words written on their awards simply state, "For great courage and skill under extremely dangerous conditions." Don Beahm echoed the sentiments of the other three when he said, "I'm really proud to be part of the group that did the rescue. I don't hold myself up as anything more than anybody else who was there. Those medals really belong to everyone."

25

"HE NEVER SAW DANGER TO HIMSELF"

March 15, 2001

New York, New York

Jeffrey Giordano

FDNY's Ladder Company 3 was formed on September 11, but a different one. The company has been in existence since 1865. The department was less than six weeks old when the company was formed. Without a doubt, the members of Ladder 3 are part of a long tradition. They have responded to many big fires over the years, but no matter what size the fire, the rescue situations comprised some of the company's most defining and heroic moments.

At about two-thirty in the morning on March 15, 2001, a fire was burning only a few blocks away from Ladder Company 3's station house. A multistory apartment building stood at 27 East 13th Street, and a fire was on the second floor in apartment 2G. Captain Patrick "Paddy" Brown (the same Patrick Brown who was involved in the Seventh Avenue rope rescue with Patrick Barr and Kevin Shea), Jeffrey Giordano, George Symon, Kevin McNamara, Chris Tighe, and Joseph Maloney were working Ladder 3 that morning.

When the truck pulled up in front of the apartment, people were on the sidewalk awaiting their arrival. Heavy smoke was coming out of some of the windows on the second floor. As soon as the truck came to a stop, the firefighters learned that a person was trapped on the second floor.

The forward entry team (FE team), composed of Captain Brown, Symon, and McNamara, jumped off the truck. Symon was on the "irons" that day, meaning that his responsibilities included making a forcible entry if needed. Firefighter Giordano was the outside vent man (OVM). His responsibility was to open the apartment from the outside to allow the smoke and heat to escape. Giordano went to the fire escape and attempted to lower the steel ladder. It was rusted in place.

As Captain Brown and his team climbed to the second floor, three engine companies arrived. Ladder 3's role was to vent the apartment and open it up for engine personnel to attack the fire with water. When they reached apartment 2G, Firefighter Symon forced the door open.

2G was the home of twenty-one-year-old Jessica Rubinstein. Inside the studio apartment, the smoke was banked nearly to the floor. A table stood to the left of the door and beyond that, a couch; a futon was on the right. Everything beyond the table was in flames.

They saw no sign of a victim. The FE team could only see fire. The kitchen area was to the right of the door. They quickly searched that area and determined that no victims were there. The engine companies were in the process of pulling hose lines, but they weren't there yet.

Outside, Giordano still had a job to do. When he couldn't access the fire escape, he retrieved a twenty-foot ladder from the truck and placed it against the building. He went up the ladder, and once at the top, he was able to look into Rubinstein's apartment. Straight ahead he could see the fire consuming most of the apartment. The only area not engulfed by flames was to his left. Jeffrey Giordano knew what he needed to do.

While standing inside the apartment, Symon heard a huge crash. "I shouldn't have been surprised. It was Jeff coming through the window. As soon as he hit the floor, he was gone. A bed was out of sight and to the right of where we were. Jeff checked the bed and couldn't find anyone at first. The fire was closing in on him, and he was out of time. Jessica Rubinstein was wedged behind the bed.

"She was unconscious and burned. He had no protection from a hose line. The heat in the back of the room was very high, and time was running out for her. He broadcast a 10-45-2, alerting the other firefighters that he had found a civilian casualty.

"I worked a lot of fires with Jeffrey, and if there was one thing for sure, he never saw danger to himself. To Giordano there was only a job to do, a mission that had to be accomplished. One time we were on this fire escape several stories up. We needed to get across to the other building, but it didn't look safe to me. Then he jumped and was on the other fire escape, just like that. Coming through the window like that was just like him."

Picking up Jessica would not have worked well. The temperature in the room was extraordinarily high. The lower Giordano stayed, the cooler it was and the less likely it was for her to be burned further. He began to drag Rubinstein back to the corner of the room, away from the flames. He intended on exiting the same way he had come in.

Seeing Giordano retreating to the corner of the room, Captain Brown moved into the room. He grabbed the kitchen table, turned it over, and used it as a shield against the flames. Brown moved through the flames and cut off the heat that was bearing down on his firefighter and the victim.

Ladder 3 didn't just have a captain working that day—they had "Paddy" Brown. His decorations for heroism were seemingly endless. He was a captain who would go through fire for his men, and he did that day. No firefighter even raised an eyebrow at Captain Brown's actions. They expected it of him because that was the kind of firefighter and man he was.

Engine 14 pulled a hose to the doorway and was able to give protection to the firefighters. With them attacking the fire, a path to the hallway was now opened and with Brown handling the table, Giordano dragged Jessica toward the doorway, where they started working on her.

Jessica's pulse was very weak and her breathing labored. She had suffered second- and third-degree burns, and her airway was shutting down because of the burns. As soon as they could, they carried her to the first floor to get away from the toxic air in the hallway.

Giordano worked to establish Jessica Rubinstein's airway. It was through his persistence that she was able to breathe. From there, she was taken to the New York Hospital burn center, where she began treatment for her burns (she was hurt badly but managed to survive). Giordano knew a lot about burn centers.

The New York Firefighters Burn Center is a nonprofit organization dedicated to providing quality care for burn patients, whether or not they have funds to pay. It is open to anyone, not just firefighters. One particular man helped out whenever he could. A late-night delivery of skin for a graft? No problem, he was there. His wife was one of the original nurses with the center and his father-in-law and uncle were both New York firefighters. Then, he too joined the FDNY, but Jeffrey Giordano still went on giving tireless service to the burn center. He eventually rose to the position of co-vice president.

Giordano's two best friends were Jim Curran and John D'Attore. Curran is the president of the burn center and D'Attore the co-vice president who remembered the commitment of his friend. "A firefighter ran 165 miles to raise money for the burn center. Jeffrey was concerned about the difficulty of the run and did the distance with him—three years in a row. He was in superior condition and ran fifteen miles a day. A normal day would see him arriving to work two hours early and he'd go for his run before his shift began."

On September 11, 2001, starting at seven o'clock in the morning, Ronzoni Macaroni sponsored a contest to determine the best Italian recipe from the FDNY. The contest was in preparation for the New York City Marathon. The winning entry would be served to all the runners the night before the big race, and Ronzoni would make a donation to the center. Giordano was among the contestants. He was off duty that day, but there to support the burn center. A little less than two hours later, a plane slammed into the North Tower of the World Trade Center.

Jeff grabbed his gear and jumped in the battalion chief's car, responding along with the other firefighters of Rescue 1. Just a few minutes before nine o'clock, he called his wife and told her he was high up in the North Tower and would be home late that day. Captain Patrick Brown and Joseph Maloney were with him. Less than an hour later they were gone, along with eight more firefighters from Rescue 1 and almost three thousand other souls.

In April of 2002, Jeffrey Giordano was posthumously awarded the number two award for heroism by *Firehouse* magazine as part of their Heroism and Community Service program. He had received many others during his distinguished career as a New York City firefighter.

Rescue 1 firefighter George Symon said, "I think of them every day. Sometimes I feel their presence in the halls or when I am on the apparatus floor. I miss them very much, we all do."

26

SEARCHING FOR BABY

August 26, 1998

Atlanta, Georgia

Wendell Porter

If you want to have uninterrupted sleep, firefighting is probably not the right job for you. In the busy houses, a twenty-four-hour shift means that many hours of work. At about 3:30 A.M. on August 26, 1998, Atlanta Firehouse 38 was awakened with a report of a house fire on Amherst Drive, in the northwest area of the city.

Ladder 38 wasn't more than three minutes from the address. When they pulled up, the large wooden-frame house was fully involved in flames. The two-story home would be reduced to a pile of embers in a matter of minutes if the Atlanta Fire Department didn't intervene.

As Firefighter Wendell Porter climbed off the ladder truck, a frantic woman ran toward the truck screaming, "Please save my baby! Please save my baby!" Although other firefighters were there, to Porter it seemed like she was speaking only to him. This wasn't going to be just any fire call. He was about to embark on an immensely profound quest,

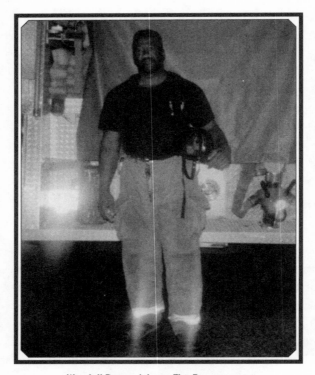
Wendell Porter, Atlanta Fire Department.

about which he would later open his heart in a poem, excerpted here, titled "Answer the Call."

I heard a mother say, "Please save my baby."
Was this my test to answer the call? Maybe!

Other people were yelling about the baby as well. The chorus of voices all confirmed that someone was trapped in the house.

He and another firefighter, Mark Hatalla, grabbed a ladder off the truck and placed it against the side of the residence. "I looked up the ladder, and flames and smoke were coming out of the window. Then I looked back at the woman."

"Please, save my baby! Please save JoJo."

Climbing the ladder into a fearful situation, Porter stopped and looked back. "The only thing I saw was the mother. I didn't see the other guys, only her standing there, calling out over and over again.

Was God testing me? Was I supposed to risk my life for someone I did not know?

That feeling inside urged me to answer the call; it seemed to say, "Just go."

And he did.

"When I got to the top of the ladder, other firefighters were calling to me and told me not to go in because they thought the floor was burned out."

Firefighters and witnesses in front of the house saw Porter slip in the window and disappear. Now all the mother could do was wait.

Entering the house through the bedroom window, the last words Porter heard was a warning not to go in. Now he faced the difficult task of locating a baby in a fog of acrid, black smoke that was so thick, in daylight your hand would be invisible directly in front of your face. But there was no daylight. Porter only knew that the baby he had been sent to save was on the second floor. JoJo was there; now he had to find him.

In the bedroom, the smoke was banked all the way to the floor. Above the smoke, flames were radiating heat down on Porter. It would later be determined that his helmet was subjected to temperatures of at

least 1,500 degrees. The nearly unbearable heat forced Porter to his
stomach on the floor.

Searching for the baby on my hands and knees,
I cried, "Dear God, please help me, please!"

Staying in a low, crawling position, Porter executed a left-hand pattern search. He had been in the room for only a minute or so, and his
turnout coat and pants were already on fire. These protective garments
are fire-retardant, but not at these temperatures. He could feel his skin
burning and his faceplate melting.

"I knew I was in the same room as the baby. I just had to figure
out where JoJo was located. The pain was almost too much. I prayed
for strength every second. I wanted to leave, but I couldn't. My air tank
was giving my back some protection, but now I was afraid it might
explode from the heat. I don't know why the room didn't flash over. I
think the flames were already there, but I just didn't see them. I'm glad
I didn't."

Outside, Porter could hear people yelling for JoJo. As he crawled,
Porter swept his hand to the side searching for a crib or bed. "The baby
had to be somewhere. I just kept checking. I didn't really know just how
bad it was for me. I was only thinking of finding him and getting out of
there. I knew I couldn't stay much longer. My face was hurting and my
hands were too."

I prayed that the baby and I would not be doomed!

"Then I touched something. It wasn't what I expected. I went in there
searching for a baby. I found JoJo, who turned out to be sixteen years
old. I learned right then as long as your mother is alive, you're always
going to be her baby, no matter how big you are."

JoJo was about five and a half feet tall and weighed about 150
pounds. "I started calling out for the other firefighters to come and help
me. After I found JoJo, I knew I had to get out of there. The heat was
really tearing me up."

I pleaded for Jesus to save my soul and get me or give me strength
to get me safely out of this.

JoJo was lying unconscious on the floor next to his bed. When Porter found the young man, he thought he could hear labored breathing. Pulling him along the floor, Porter headed for the window.

"I yelled, 'I found him. I found him. Help! Help! I need help. I found him.' I knew the way I had come, and I went back toward the window. I had to stay down on the floor as I went because of the heat and fire just above me. I was in terrible pain, but I wasn't leaving JoJo behind. If he was going to have any chance, it would be with me pulling him out right then. If I waited for the flames and heat to be knocked down, it would be too late for him. Even though it was a short distance back to the window, it seemed like forever.

"Finally, I got back to the window with JoJo. He was totally limp. I didn't think about what condition he was in then. All I was interested in was getting us both out of there. I expected the room to flash over any second. I still couldn't see a thing. I knew there was a firefighter on the ladder, but I didn't know who it was.

"I had to lift JoJo up to get him out to the firefighter on the ladder. I got on my hands and knees and managed to get him over my shoulder. Then I raised myself up. When I stood up, I went right into the fire. I held onto the window with one hand, and I had him with the other. The flames and heat were getting me pretty good then.

"I almost lost him when I got him up there, it was close. I was calling out to the other guys to take him and he slipped and started to go out the window. I thought the other firefighter had him, but he didn't and I grabbed JoJo and pulled him back."

Suddenly, a ball of fire blew through the window as a firefighter went down the ladder with JoJo. The firefighters below realized with horror that it was Wendell Porter. In the process of jumping, his glove came off, and with it came much of his skin.

"I couldn't wait to use the ladder. I had to leave. I thought I broke my leg when I hit, but that was the least of my worries."

Lieutenant Michael Holtzclaw and Hatalla ran to Porter and started ripping off his protective gear, causing the lieutenant to receive second-degree burns for his efforts. Porter had second- and third-degree burns on his face, neck, ears, shoulders, arms, hands, and back. Outside, in the air, the pain really hit him. "It was incredible. They were pouring water on me, trying to stop the progress of the burns. I was yelling at them to take the water off me and when they did, the pain was even worse so I told them 'Put some more on, put some more on.' "

His turnout pants and jacket were burned, his faceplate was melted to his face, and his helmet had disintegrated. The helmet manufacturer later marveled that Porter didn't collapse and die in the house. They had never seen heat damage that severe on a helmet where the firefighter left the structure under his own power.

Another battle was now underway. Wendell Porter was in critical condition and on his way to the hospital burn center. En route, he drifted in and out of consciousness. The following night he was alert enough to talk to people. It was then that he learned JoJo had died. The combination of extreme temperatures and poisonous gases with little or no oxygen had been too much for the young man. Lying in his hospital bed, Porter cried. He also prayed, thanking God for sparing him.

He had saved my life, although my body was burned.

Two and a half months later, Porter was released from the hospital. After several skin-graft operations, he returned to full duty a year later.

Wendell Porter received medals of valor from the city of Atlanta, Atlanta Metropolitan Firefighters Association, Atlanta Association of Insurance Women, and his fraternity, Omega Psi Phi, at Middle Tennessee State University. Middle Tennessee State University also awarded Porter with the Black Alumni Achievement Award. Georgia's governor granted Porter a special Medal of Valor and he was also the Atlanta Firefighter of the Year. In the finest tradition of the firefighting service, he had risked almost certain death in his quest to save the life of another human being.

I pray the next time there is a call to answer, I am found worthy of answering the call.

Those who know Wendell Porter don't worry about that question.